TEN PRESIDENTS AND THE PRESS

Edited by

Kenneth W. Thompson

UNIVERSITY
PRESS OF
AMERICA

LANHAM • NEW YORK • LONDON

TEN PRESIDENTS AND THE PRESS

VOLUME III IN A SERIES
FUNDED BY THE
JOHN and MARY R. MARKLE FOUNDATION

Copyright © 1983 by

University Press of America,™ Inc.

4720 Boston Way
Lanham, MD 20706

3 Henrietta Street
London WC2E 8LU England

Printed in the United States of America

Library of Congress Cataloging in Publication Data

Main entry under title:

Ten presidents and the press.

  "White Burkett Miller Center of Public Affairs at
the University of Virginia."
  Bibliography: p.
  1. Presidents—United States—History—20th century—
Congresses. 2. Press and politics—United States—
History—20th century—Congresses. 3. United States—
Politics and government—20th century—Congresses.
I. Thompson, Kenneth W., 1921-   . II. White Burkett
Miller Center.
E176.1.T43   1983   353.03'5   82-20293
ISBN 0-8191-2877-5
ISBN 0-8191-2878-3 (pbk.)

All University Press of America books are produced on acid-free
paper which exceeds the minimum standards set by the National
Historical Publications and Records Commission.

TEN PRESIDENTS
AND THE PRESS

Dedicated
to the
memory
of
Frank W. Rogers, Sr., Esq.
(1892–1982)

TABLE OF CONTENTS

PREFACE

In 1979, the White Burkett Miller Center of the University of Virginia chose as an important program interest the study of the presidency and the press. With support from the John and Mary R. Markle Foundation, its first effort was the establishment of a national commission co-chaired by Linwood Holton, former Governor of Virginia and Chairman of the Council of the Miller Center, and Ray Scherer, Vice President of RCA. Its work culminated in the announcement of press secretary James Brady that President Reagan intended to follow the recommendations set forth in the commission's report in the conduct of his press conferences.

A second project of the Center was the support and publication of a book on the history of presidential press conferences by a brilliant young scholar, Blaire French. This brief history has been praised as a model of cogency and clarity in historical and political analysis.

The present volume is the third publication in the series. It brings together the work of leading presidential interpreters and scholars who met for extended discussions at the Miller Center. It contains presentations and discussions on ten presidents and their relations with the press: Woodrow Wilson, Franklin D. Roosevelt, Harry S. Truman, Dwight D. Eisenhower, John F. Kennedy, Lyndon B. Johnson, Richard M. Nixon, Gerald Ford, Jimmy Carter, and Ronald Reagan.

The Center intends to complete its work on presidential press conferences through the publication of a volume on practical issues in presidential-press corps relations.

INTRODUCTION

The contributors to this volume are well-known commentators on the presidency. Each is uniquely qualified to appraise the particular president or presidents they were invited to discuss.

Professor George Juergens is a member of the History Department at the University of Indiana and an authority on Woodrow Wilson and the press. His recent book on Wilson is to be followed by a book on F.D.R. Juergens' work has been recognized by various foundations and scholarly organizations.

Chalmers Roberts has been a senior columnist for the *Washington Post* who has reported on a number of presidents. The role he played at the center of the debate regarding release of the Pentagon Papers has been widely discussed. He is especially well-qualified to discuss the Franklin D. Roosevelt presidency from a broad historical perspective.

Robert Donovan is the foremost biographer of Harry S. Truman, now engaged in completing volume two in that important work. He has served as a respected columnist, a press secretary, and a researcher and teacher at leading universities, including Princeton. In his discussion of President Truman and the press, he goes beyond the subject matter of his biography, to discuss Truman's unique style of relating to the press.

Ray Scherer covered the White House for NBC during the Eisenhower presidency and observed important changes in press conferences brought about by the introduction of television. Scherer, who is Vice President of RCA, has been instrumental in the organization and guidance of Miller Center staff in the press conference project.

Charles Roberts, recently retired from the staff of *Newsweek*, had a close personal relationship with John F. Kennedy. He

1

discusses the beginning of a new era in political communication which he witnessed during the brief but inspiring Kennedy presidency.

Carroll Kilpatrick, retired columnist of the *Washington Post*, covered both the Lyndon B. Johnson and Richard M. Nixon presidencies. His calm and thoughtful assessments of these two presidents adds an important chapter to the study of the relation of the president and the press. Like Scherer, Kilpatrick has had an ongoing association with the Miller Center.

Ray Scherer then concludes the volume with comments on Presidents Ford, Carter, and Reagan. The full record of President Reagan's press relations was not available at the time of this discussion. It is possible that Scherer would wish to add to his comments if his paper had been written on the date of publication of this volume.

Additional participants included James Latimer, the dean of commentators on state politics for the *Richmond Times Dispatch*; Staige Blackford, editor of the *Virginia Quarterly Review*; Felicia Warburg Rogan, member of the Center's National Commission on the Presidential Press Conference; Mr. James Young, director of the Program on the Presidency of the Miller Center; and Charles O. Jones, Professor of Government of the University of Virginia.

The discussion which follows is reproduced essentially as it occurred in November of 1981.

Kenneth W. Thompson
Director

THOMPSON: We're grateful and pleased that you could join us in this small group to undertake a review of two areas. We want in the first place to look back, as in a sense we did in the Presidential Press Conference project, but never systematically, to particular presidents. Maybe we were less systematic because the Miller Center was dealing with what may have been for the staff a new breed of professionals. A younger colleague passed on a few comments about your profession that may be all too familiar to you. Rebecca West wrote, "Journalism is the ability to meet the challenge of filling space." Lord Northcliffe wrote, "Journalism: a profession whose business it is to explain to others what it personally doesn't understand." Adlai Stevenson: "Newspaper editors are men who separate the wheat from the chaff and then print the chaff. . . . " *The Left Handed Dictionary*: "Journalist: A near-sighted historian." And finally, the only complimentary reference to your field, by de Tocqueville, as you might have guessed: "The only authors whom I acknowledge as American are the journalists—they, indeed, are not great writers but they speak the language of their countrymen and make themselves heard by them." Perhaps that's one of the reasons that of all the projects the Miller Center has undertaken the Presidential Press Conference project evoked the most public response and public reaction.

Today we'd like to look back at particular presidents to find out what their relationship was with the press, how they approached communication, what they had to say about the overall subject, and what scholars and writers have discovered in their contacts and relationships with the press. In this way we hope that we at the Miller Center may have something additional to share with a concerned public and with those who have made possible this project, the Markle Foundation.

WOODROW WILSON

THOMPSON: Professor George Juergens is a leading historian at Indiana University. He is undertaking a major review of the presidency and the press and has published a first book on the progressive presidents. He is continuing his work with a second volume on Franklin D. Roosevelt. He has had grants from a number of foundations, including the Rockefeller Foundation. We thought since we may not have done Woodrow Wilson justice, or the period he represents, that it would be good to start out with a discussion of Wilson and the press.

JUERGENS: Thank you, Dr. Thompson, and thank you for inviting me to participate in this session at the Miller Center. It's a pleasure to be here.

In discussing Woodrow Wilson's dealings with the press, it seems to me that we have to balance contradictory themes. On the one hand, he was a brilliant publicist, someone whose effectiveness in advertising himself and his causes made him a dominating political presence in the Progressive era. In the sense of using publicity as a vehicle for power, he easily belongs with Theodore Roosevelt and Franklin Roosevelt as one of the giants who laid the foundation for the modern presidency. On the other hand, throughout his public career Wilson was handicapped by an inability to adjust to the demands of popular journalism, and even by a blindness as to what the role of the press is in a democracy. For a long while he succeeded in compensating for those weaknesses. In the end, as I will argue, they contributed to his defeat on the issue he cared about above all others: American involvement in the League of Nations.

What caused the abrasions between Wilson and reporters? How did he manage to adjust? Why did the abrasions matter in the long run? These are the questions I propose to address in the time available to me. I hope in our discussion later my comments will have some bearing on the presidency of today.

A way to start is to say that in one sense the problem between Wilson and the press was as complicated as human personality itself. Bear in mind that we speak about a figure who had been involved in politics for barely a year when he set out to win his party's presidential nomination. A lifetime spent as a college professor and college president—and at Princeton, no less, hardly one of your places for the *hoi polloi*—was not the best preparation for dealing with reporters whose police court origins were not that far behind them. They were a down-to-earth lot, even boisterous on occasion, who looked for the common touch in the men they covered. They admired colorfulness more than dignity, horse sense more than high-flown wisdom. Wilson had never met their kind at Princeton and didn't know quite what to make of them. Part of the reason he and the press clashed is that they were strangers to one another.

Their differences could easily have been bridged, however, but for the more serious problem of Wilson's austere personality. He was a man of enormous reserve, one who without intending it gave the impression of somehow being apart from the rest of humanity. Even at his best moments, the quality of remoteness was always there. As one historian has pointed out, Wilson enjoyed great popularity as a teacher at Princeton, but for his ability in lecturing to large groups, not in handling the give and take of small classes. As a political leader he moved audiences with his eloquence; he rarely warmed them by his presence. The contrast between Americans calling Theodore Roosevelt "Teddy" (a nickname he detested, by the way) but Woodrow Wilson seldom "Woody" conveys the difference. He was not the sort of person newsmen would naturally take to, nor the sort who would even try to win them over.

Compound personal differences with clash over news values and the problem deepens. The disagreement took many forms. In its most mundane aspect—but no less deeply and bitterly felt for all that—it had to do with coverage of the Wilson family. The issue, of course, is a perennial one in American life. Presidents, like anyone else, want some privacy; at the same time public interest in the family that fills an almost symbolic role has the press constantly digging for more information and, when the information is not freely given, making do with speculation about what might be. The result is invariably tension between presidents and the press. In Wilson's case, however, the tension reached unprecedented heights because of the kind of man he was. His reserve and high sense of dignity would have made this aspect of public life an ordeal even if he alone had been in the spotlight. He nearly cracked upon seeing his beloved wife and daughters subjected to the treatment. Wilson, after all, was a Southerner. He worshiped women in the old-fashioned way, thinking of them as innately pure and finer creatures to be shielded from the world outside. It was almost more than he could bear to have what he regarded as the coarse and ill-mannered denizens of the press hounding his ladies, and as if that were not enough, speculating about their personal affairs in public print.

The troubles began immediately after Wilson's nomination when a horde of reporters descended on his summer home in Sea Girt, New Jersey, looking for human interest material on the candidate's wife and daughters. The Wilsons, all of them, were pathetically unprepared for the persistence and brazeness of the questioning. As the President's middle daughter, Eleanor, recalled,

> We, who had been taught to be closed-mouthed about our family affairs, found this prying into our lives strange and annoying. They did not hesitate to question us about any and every detail of our lives. What were our favorite colors, occupation, sports? Did we like to dance? Were we in love or engaged? Did we intend to marry and, if so, when?

The loyal Eleanor traced her father's troubles with the press to the trauma of those first interviews. As she wrote, "He resented almost fiercely the attempts to pry into family affairs and tried to protect us as much as he could. I've always believed that the first rumors of his 'aloofness' and 'unfriendliness' were the result of his annoyance at this first onslaught upon us." Perhaps, and then again, perhaps not. The important point is that the onslaught never stopped, and Wilson—who had to suffer in coming years through press coverage of two daughters' engagements and weddings, the concert career of a third daughter, the illness and death of his wife, the courtship of Mrs. Galt and controversial marriage to her—never got over his bitterness against prying reporters.

Wilson's misunderstanding, or perhaps it was stubbornness, about another way in which journalism works caused still more tensions between him and White House correspondents. He thought of news as the announcement of a decision made or a step taken, which it was the responsibility of the press to convey without comment or interpolation. Reporters, as far as he was concerned, had no business speculating about what might happen, or printing information before it had been officially released. Of course newspapers run on that basis would be little more than bulletins for the administration in power. The responsibility for keeping the public informed assumes that stories will often be published that government leaders would prefer to remain under wraps. It also assumes that reporters will enter the picture while decisions are being made so that the people can have some voice in the process, rather than always being presented with a *fait accompli*. Wilson was hardly unique among presidents in wanting the press to be little more than a conveyor belt passing along his statements as provided. But he more than most chose to make an issue of the matter, and in the process deepened the chill in his relations with reporters.

Again, the troubles started even before the inauguration. Wilson was enraged, for example, to the extent of blowing up altogether at a couple of press briefings because of the attempts by newsmen to ferret out the names of his cabinet appointees before he was ready to make the announcement. Indeed, like Lyndon Johnson decades later, he gave the press something of a veto power over who found places in the administration—an unwelcome power, I might add—by refusing to follow through on appointments if newspapers got wind of the names first.

Still another area of contention—one that may have mattered most of all—was the sense among reporters that Wilson's word could not be trusted. They felt early on, and became more convinced with the passage of time, that the things he said to them were often calculated to deceive. Not that he typically engaged in outright lies. Wilson's usual tactic when he wanted to throw up a smokescreen was to respond with the truth, but the truth expressed in such a way that listeners could easily be fooled. "It was impossible to rely on anything he said," a *New York Times* reporter wrote (incidentally, the reporter happened to be a Wilson admirer). "I do not mean he lied. I mean that he took such an intellectual pleasure in stating a thing so as to give an opposite impression to the fact, though he kept strictly to the truth, that one had to be constantly on the alert to keep from being misled." The problem with playing Wilson's kind of "intellectual" game is that it made him too clever by half in the eyes of the press. Reporters then as now are likely to put up with any number of peccadillos in public figures, and perhaps even be amused by them. What they cannot accept is a politician, particularly when he is President of the United States, whose word cannot be accepted at face value. Wilson struck them as such a man.

All of which is to say that by the time of his inauguration in March 1913, Woodrow Wilson was thoroughly disillusioned with the press, and the press thoroughly disillusioned with Woodrow Wilson. Indeed, I can think of no twentieth century president—with the obvious exception of Richard Nixon, in all things a story unto himself—who entered office more estranged from working reporters.

It is ironic, considering that one of his first steps as President was to institute regular press conferences at the White House, an innovation that did much to enhance the status of Washington correspondents, and that for decades afterwards provided the mechanism for frequent contact between presidents and press. The further irony is that he took the step in large part because of how he felt about reporters.

The seeming contradiction is easily explained. Wilson was much too shrewd a student of government to underestimate the importance of publicity for the person who presides in the Oval Office. Long before he entered public life he had made the point in several scholarly works that leadership in a democracy depends on the ability to influence public opinion. At one time he assumed that the legislative branch, being closer to the people, could do it best. His thought changed, largely under the influence of Theodore Roosevelt's presidency, when he recognized the unique opportunities available to a president to get his message across. As he wrote in *Constitutional Government in the United States*, published in 1908, " ... that part of the government which has the most direct access to opinion has the best chance of leadership and mastery; and at present that part is the President." With his own election the moral was inescapable. To be a strong president he would have to rally the people behind him, explaining to them what he was trying to accomplish in order to win their support. And since the newspaper represented his primary medium of communication, it made sense to do what he could to influence what appeared about him in newspapers.

By the same token he also knew that he couldn't manage his press relations in the way Theodore Roosevelt had, by seeing reporters almost every day, either individually or in small groups, for personal chats. Aside from the physical strain, and Wilson had never been a robust individual, it seemed silly to have to repeat his points over and over again in individual conversations. He might have felt differently if, like Roosevelt, he had enjoyed the company of newsmen. In that case, seeing them could be a welcome break in the daily routine. But since he didn't like most newsmen, he needed a different way to stay in touch with them while minimizing the aggravation they caused him. The press conference, an idea most likely suggested to him by his secretary, Joseph Tumulty, provided the answer. He would strive to lead public opinion by meeting regularly each week with reporters to answer their questions, which presumably were the questions on the minds of the citizenry. At the same time, he would keep reporters at least somewhat at a distance by seeing them all at once, and pretty well restricting his availability to these formal and, he hoped, businesslike sessions. Respect for the people he would be meeting with had nothing to do with the decision. If anything, he made the move despite his feelings about journalists.

All things considered, perhaps it is not surprising that the conferences never worked well. Wilson was appalled by the petty, personal, uninformed questions many reporters asked. In fairness to him, he dealt with a press corps far less educated and qualified than Washington correspondents of today, and he often had good reason to be upset. So did he resent the attempts by newsmen to badger him into making information available before he was ready to do so. They never seemed to learn that he intended to be the one to decide what news got out and when. He felt particularly strongly on the matter in foreign affairs, an area where as far as he was concerned the press could only cause mischief, and therefore had no business intruding. It didn't lead to notably fruitful exchanges in the conferences.

There was always a very cool reserve, (a former associate wrote) and

Wilson gave the impression that he was the best judge of what was proper for the newspapers to have. He was saving mankind, and he would let the world know about it in his own good time. He certainly did not believe in government by newspapers, and it was his policy that the newspapers should not know of any transaction until it was accomplished.

If the President's failure to be forthcoming hardly endeared him to the press, his air of aloof superiority did nothing to help matters. To their annoyance, the reporters felt like schoolboys apprehensive about being in the presence of a haughty headmaster. Worse, they got the sense (reading Wilson correctly as it turned out) that he didn't regard them as particularly bright pupils. It is one thing to be treated with chill formality, and another to be cast as a dullard. Wilson had a way of doing that, to the discomfort of experienced journalists as well as those just starting out.

Perhaps the fundamental problem, underlying all others, was that Wilson had little sense of how to structure the conferences to serve his publicity purposes. He rarely used opening statements to generate news and suggest a line of inquiry for reporters to follow. He didn't plant questions with cooperative newsmen. By and large he didn't excel at turning questions around to hold forth on what he really wanted to discuss. His press conferences belonged mainly to the reporters to do with as they liked. When he didn't approve of the direction in which they wanted to go, which was most of the time, he simply clammed up.

Considering the hard feelings these sessions caused for all concerned, it is little wonder that they came to a limping end. Wilson started out by meeting the press twice a week. Twenty-one months into his administration, in December 1914, he cut back to one conference a week. Seven months later, in July 1915, seizing on the *Lusitania* crisis as an excuse, he abandoned the experiment altogether. The press conferences lasted less than two-and-a-half years out of the eight years of Wilson's presidency. After dropping them he met with reporters in a body on only three occasions in the second term to urge support for the League of Nations.

My point is not to minimize the significance of Wilson's experiment. He established a precedent that his successor in the White House came back to, and then the next president, and the president following. By the time Franklin Roosevelt had completed twelve years in office, holding to a remarkably consistent schedule of two meetings a week with reporters, the conferences had ceased to be an option available to presidents and developed as an important institution in their own right; an institution that many observers, incorrectly I believe, went so far as to compare to the parliamentary question period in Great Britain.

The fact remains that Wilson, the president who started it all, derived little publicity benefit himself from the conferences. If anything, they may on balance have been a liability in exacerbating his already strained relationship with reporters. This human dimension in the dealings between presidents and the press should not be ignored. What I'm about to say might be challenged later, but it seems to me that while a personally popular president may receive rough treatment at the hands of journalists (Harry Truman is perhaps an example), the chances of a personally unpopular president receiving favorable treatment are much more remote. In those cases the judgments about performance in office are colored, necessarily so, by the dislike for the sort of man he is. For the great majority of reporters, Wilson's conferences succeeded mainly in confirming how much they in fact disliked him.

And yet for most of his years in office he received a good press. What did he have going for him? It didn't hurt that he came to office at a time of relative prosperity, and presided over a popular program, and succeeded with great political skill in getting that program enacted. William Howard Taft, by contrast, lost enormous credibility in the first months of his administration by failing to deliver on the promise of tariff reform. Wilson showed he was made of different stuff by barely settling into the Oval Office before he had taken on the lobbyists and pressured Congress into passing the Underwood Tariff, the first significant reduction in duties since the Civil War. It is extremely difficult to take potshots at the man in the White House when the people are happy with what he is doing, and contented with their own lot in life.

Wilson's formidable skills as an orator provided a further source of strength. Through the spoken word he was able, at least to an extent, to reach out directly to the public and pretty well require that the press pay respectful attention. Particularly

11

when he did something so dramatic as revive a practice that had been abandoned since John Adams by appearing periodically in person to address the joint houses of Congress. It was impossible not to give such speeches saturation coverage. The country was fascinated. And once he had the attention of the national audience, Wilson demonstrated time and again his ability to elevate the spirit through noble thoughts eloquently expressed. Reporters, even if they disliked him could do little against that kind of clout.

During the first term, before his fall from influence, Joseph Tumulty also helped a great deal. Part of the reason is that reporters liked Tumulty just about as much as they disliked his boss. In almost every respect he was Wilson's opposite as a human being (which is odd considering the close bond between the two men). To a legion of admirers, Tumulty summed up everything best in the stereotypical figure of the warm-hearted Irishman. He was funloving, witty, marvelous at telling Irish-dialect stories, generous, compassionate. Tumulty performed many publicity functions for the President. He conducted daily briefings for the press, and with great skill. He knew how to pace the news, how to build up forthcoming events, how to float trial balloons, how to milk all the drama out of a human interest story. Wilson used him as a sounding board for his speeches, and relied heavily on his deft reading of trends in public opinion. Perhaps his foremost contribution, however, and also the one most difficult to pin down, was simply in making friends of Washington correspondents. As a surrogate the secretary could only accomplish so much, but he was able to say, in effect, to reporters, "Come on, the old man's not so bad," and have some influence. So the correspondents recognized, themselves, in the words of one of them who covered the White House at the time, "There is no use denying that 'Joe' puts over many a thing that [would be treated differently] lacking the power of the personal equation."

Finally, American involvement in World War I gave Wilson an enormous publicity advantage. It was not simply that national leaders tend to be beyond criticism when the wars they preside over are going well, although that factor weighed heavily enough. With the establishment of the Committee on Public Information to handle government propaganda, the executive branch did something that had never been done before, and that Congress would specifically forbid the Office of War Information from trying again during World War II. Under George Creel, the Committee pitched its message about American unity and idealism and purpose around the figure of Woodrow Wilson, Commander-in-Chief. Boy Scouts were enlisted to distribute millions of copies of his speeches door to door. Every teacher in the country, 600,000 of them, received a biweekly newspaper from the Committee with suggestions on how to incorporate the theme of Wilsonian idealism into the school curriculum. The so-called "Four Minute Men" delivered over one million talks on the same theme at movie houses and churches and social clubs, reaching an estimated total audience of four hundred million people (which is not bad considering that the population of the country at the time was only one hundred million). For nineteen months of war Woodrow Wilson symbolized the goodness and inner convictions of America. Which is to say, he stood above politics on a plateau hitherto reserved for presidents safely dead. You can't ask for better publicity than that.

And yet, in the end, publicity—or more precisely, estrangement from the working press—contributed to his downfall. By the time he went to Paris to negotiate the treaty that he hoped would end all wars, many of the old sources of strength were gone. At the insistence of Congress the Committee on Public Information was forced to rapidly dismantle its operations. Joseph Tumulty had long since been stripped of his publicity function, and if the second Mrs. Wilson and Colonel Edward House, the President's chief aide, had their way, he would have been forced out of the administration altogether. (Mrs. Wilson regarded Tumulty as common and vulgar; not the sort of person a refined man like her husband should have as a close associate. She also bitterly resented that Tumulty had urged the President to put off remarrying until after the 1916 election.) At this juncture not even the magic with words offered much of an advantage. Wilson obviously could not address his countrymen from three thousand miles away, and in any event by 1919 the years had taken their physical toll and he was no longer the orator he had once been.

The moral was inescapable. To win support for his cherished League of Nations the President had no choice but to put old animosities behind him and work closely with reporters, explaining to them the importance of American involvement in the League so that their dispatches might, in turn, educate the country. This he failed to do. Instead, he acquiesced in the news blackout that poisoned the atmosphere at the Peace Conference, and encouraged a drumbeat of negative dispatches back to the United States. His aides recognized what was happening and pleaded with him to repair the damage by making himself available to the press. He refused, partly because time in Paris was precious and the strength for any extra chore just about nonexistent, and partly because he thought that if necessary he could rally the country by going on a speaking tour once he returned home.

It is a nice question whether minds are won that easily, but we never found out. You all know what happened. Wilson suffered a stroke on the tour that forced him to cancel his remaining engagements and rush back to Washington. A second massive stroke a few days after his return crippled him. During the long ratification struggle in the Senate, many reporters got their revenge against a president they resented by cooperating actively with the Irreconcilables in lobbying against the treaty. Public opinion, which had started out cautiously in favor of the League, slowly turned. In November 1919, the Treaty and the League it encompassed were decisively rejected. The education conducted over many months in newspapers that might have made the difference never took place. Wilson's tragic inability to work at first hand with reporters finally mattered.

KILPATRICK: I'd like to say I thought it was a superb paper. I thought I knew a little about Wilson but I certainly didn't know anything about his press operation. I thought that Lyndon Johnson and Wilson were the two most opposite presidents in every way, and now I find that there is a great parallel.

JUERGENS: There are certain parallels, although I think of Lyndon Johnson as a rather crude man and, whatever we would say about Wilson, he wasn't crude. One of the problems we have is that the transcripts of the conferences are not complete. They are more like minutes than verbatim transcripts, so it's difficult to say exactly who asked what and how he was answered. But as you read through those transcripts, it's remarkable to what extent in conference after conference virtually nothing of substance was said.

SCHERER: He didn't use it to make news? He didn't come in with announcements?

JUERGENS: No, and that's an important point. I happen to believe that the first president who knew how to do that, and he remains perhaps the all-time champion at the art, was Franklin Roosevelt. But Wilson knew nothing about using opening statements as a way to make news and to influence what questions he would be asked. Now, I don't think we can speak in black and white terms. There were one or two occasions where he did use the press conference effectively. One occasion in particular comes to mind, although I think it's revealing that it was very early in his presidency, in the first six to eight weeks. Some reporter asked him about the revolution in Mexico, and on this occasion Wilson had the good sense to respond, "Look, why don't you ask a good question? Why don't you ask a question about something closer to home? Ask me a question about all these lobbyists who are descending on Washington trying to defeat tariff reform. You can't throw a brick without hitting one of them." He then held forth on the lobbyists and generated good news. That's a case of his using conferences the way they could be used, but there were only a few such occasions in his presidency.

SCHERER: What was the physical setting? Was he seated at his desk in the Oval Office?

JUERGENS: He sometimes received the press standing behind his desk, but he also used the East Room.

LATIMER: Were there any ground rules about direct quotes?

JUERGENS: You couldn't quote him directly unless he gave formal permission, and then he preferred the quote to come in a written release. In this regard, his practice was very close to Franklin Roosevelt's. On the occasion with the lobbyists, for example, when the reporters asked for permission to quote him, he said, "Well, I'll give you something in a little while." He wrote out the answer and had Tumulty issue it as a release. Otherwise the correspondents had to use indirect attribution. But at least they could cite the President as their source. The "White House spokesmen" euphemism didn't come along until the Coolidge years.

LATIMER: How big were these conferences? About how many people were there?

JUERGENS: The first two conferences drew an enormous number of people—well over a hundred, getting close to two hundred—which was remarkable considering the size of the press corps in 1913. Many reporters, including some who were close to Wilson, said that he seemed to be almost appalled by the size of the turnout. He gave the impression of being taken aback at seeing all of those people present. Of course, as the conferences became what they became, attendance dropped precipitously, and toward the end you'd have maybe twenty people showing up.

SCHERER: I'd like to pose the question of whether Wilson would have been more effective if he had had radio or television. The new technology, would it have made a difference? He seemed to have a particular animus toward the writing press and looked down his nose at them.

JUERGENS: Of course there's no way of knowing, but there are historians who argue that if he had had radio rather than having to go on that speaking tour, it might have made a difference regarding American involvement in the League. After all, he was a marvelous speaker, and for purposes of argument we can assume that he would have been as effective on radio as he was on the public platform. I don't know. Here I must defer to you gentlemen, but I tend to be dubious. It strikes me that you don't change minds overnight. I think that a selling campaign, particularly on something as profound as America changing its whole history by entering the League of Nations, would have required more than three or four radio talks. And he couldn't have done more than three or four without dissipating their impact. I think the job was something that has to be accomplished over months. After all, he had to deal with senators who are elected for six years. Even if Wilson impressed some of their constituents back home, senators have a certain staying power to resist constituent pressure. In order to win, Wilson would have had to start the selling campaign early in 1919; instead, he waited until the end of the summer.

SCHERER: The curious thing that comes out in your presentation is how this mutual personal animus was apparently heavily reflected in what they wrote, and they actively got in league with the opposing senators. He then began to look on the press as an enemy.

JUERGENS: I gather that when American reporters went

to Paris, although there was the long history of animus between them and the President, for reasons of simple patriotism they were ready to write pro-Wilson articles. All the more because when they got there they saw a French press that struck them as a captive press. From the beginning they yearned to be spoken to so that they could present the American side. That in a way compounded their disillusionment; they wanted to help and they couldn't. Of course there was also the disillusionment in taking the first of fourteen points literally. It was probably naive of them, but they thought that Wilson literally meant "open covenants openly arrived at." They seemed to think that somehow the press would be covering secret conversations between Lloyd George and Wilson. So there was a sense of betrayal. Far from having open covenants openly arrived at, the conference was closed down to them. Whatever news came out, came out through leaks. The results were reports from Paris that in effect said—and I think this hurt—"It's not a brave new world; it's the same old thing of secret diplomacy for selfish gains." What I am trying to suggest is that Wilson needed publicity on the theme, "We're in the process of building something that mankind has never attempted before, an international organization." Instead he got news reports that told America, "It's the same old game."

BLACKFORD: But in fact, that is what it was. It was Smuts who said tht the Treaty of Versailles is the peace that passeth understanding.

JUERGENS: I think it was also a peace treaty that fell between every considerable stool. I think that Wilson undoubtedly was trying to build a new world—

BLACKFORD: Lloyd George and Clemenceau weren't.

JUERGENS: No, they weren't, but of course he tugged them and they tugged him, and that's how you ended up between stools.

THOMPSON: Do any of his press conferences show what Keynes and others were later to criticize him for on the Peace Treaty, lack of interest in detail? Was that any problem with reporters?

JUERGENS: Bear in mind that he had only two or three conferences in the second term, so there were only two or three that would touch on the Treaty at all. One of those conferences he held just before he sailed back to the United States for a visit midway through the conference. He met with reporters at the dockside, and responded rather flippantly to a question of enormous emotional significance at the time. He was asked about the freedom of the seas point, and he said in a kidding way,

> Well, I suddenly realized when I got here that the joke's on me. The freedom of the seas issue is irrelevant because you only have to worry about freedom of the seas when you don't have an international organization, and we're going to have the League of Nations. So freedom of the seas isn't a problem.

Someone asked him if the British gave him that line, a sort of hostile question, and he laughed and said, "No, I thought that one up all by myself." The point is that the dispatches about the press conference suggested that on an issue of enormous importance to most Americans—after all, we'd gotten into the war because of freedom of the seas—Wilson was being a little cavalier.

BLACKFORD: I have an essay by John Milton Cooper called "Woodrow Wilson: The Academic Man" in which he points out that Wilson really didn't have all that much interest in detail, that he was not of the real Johns Hopkins/German school of scholarship and he did not really like working with graduate students. I was wondering if this academic background could have any effect on his later relations with the press?

JUERGENS: Well, I think it did from the point of view of making him excessively cultured in the eyes of the press. But you're quite right; I also think there's a great myth about Wilson. We think of Wilson the intellectual, Wilson the scholar. That's not altogether so. He wrote his doctoral dissertation on Congress while at Johns Hopkins, in Baltimore, and in the writing of it never once went to Washington to research on the spot what Congress was actually about. He wasn't interested in that sort of detail. When the book was published, his fiancee—who became the first Mrs. Wilson—wrote to him saying, "You should feel triumphant. Why are you so depressed?" And he wrote back to her, "I don't want this. Scholarship doesn't interest me. I want to lead people." Theodore Roosevelt was in many ways an intellectual; he read voraciously and widely. Woodrow Wilson pretty well confined himself to detective novels.

SCHERER: Did the relationship between Wilson and the whole press corps go sour? Did he not have one defender? One single columnist?

JUERGENS: Yes. Here, once again, in the short time available I'm making things too one-sided. There were certainly people who respected him. Richard Oulahan covered him for the *New York Times*, and there was sentiment on the paper that he should be relieved of the assignment because he struck some editors as excessively pro-Wilson. Walter Lippmann and Wilson also respected each other. Wilson regarded Lippmann as a bright man. He didn't think of all newsmen as nincompoops, and several of the correspondents respected Wilson in turn.

KILPATRICK: But Lippmann at the time was not an active correspondent; he was really working for Wilson most of that time.

JUERGENS: He joined the government in World War I.

THOMPSON: Then he broke.

KILPATRICK: He was a great admirer and then he broke. Would you agree that in talking about Wilson's not taking the press into his confidence while he was in Paris, his contempt for the press was one factor, and another was his feeling that he could always go out on the stump and sway the people with a great speech? He could get home and he could turn things around.

JUERGENS: That was a major factor, and something I didn't hit hard enough, a third factor is that Wilson believed that the press had no business covering a subject until the decisions had been made. He felt particularly strongly in that regard when it came to foreign affairs. Right along he felt that all the press can do in writing about foreign affairs before the agreement is made is muck things up. So if he kept reporters at arm's length, one of the reasons is that he thought it would be poison to bring them in.

KILPATRICK: Or the Senate into it.

JUERGENS: Or the Senate.

KILPATRICK: That was the fatal error.

JUERGENS: That hurt a lot.

DONOVAN: May I ask a question? How much influence do you think the second Mrs. Wilson had in Paris, in keeping him away from the press?

JUERGENS: I think she had a certain influence, because bear in mind, he may have suffered a stroke in Paris, and was certainly dreadfully ill. Several accounts describe as almost pathetic the scene of him emerging from the working sessions. Lloyd George would stalk out hale and hearty, while Wilson could barely make it to a couch before he had to sit down to catch his breath. My point is that Mrs. Wilson was concerned first of all with protecting her husband's health. It wasn't only the press. She wanted to keep everybody away from him as much as possible, including key members of the American delegation, so he would have a chance to rest. I think that was a factor.

JONES: I wondered whether he viewed the magazine people any differently from the newspaper people, or were these the same people at this time?

JUERGENS: They were essentially the same people, and I'm not sure that he viewed them differently.

THOMPSON: We've been told that Teddy Roosevelt called the reporters in from the rain, and that began the press conference. Is there any substantiation of that in Wilson's explanation of where he got the idea?

JUERGENS: No. He seems to have hit upon the idea independently, with Tumulty perhaps providing a nudge. I think, though, that Theodore Roosevelt had an enormous influence upon Wilson. The two men were great rivals and Wilson chortled any time he came up with something that Theodore Roosevelt hadn't thought about. But what Theodore Roosevelt did teach Wilson was that if you're imaginative you can own the headlines. And owning the headlines means power. Theodore Roosevelt redefined for Wilson the nature of American government in demonstrating the publicity powers of the presidency.

FRANKLIN DELANO ROOSEVELT

THOMPSON: Now let's begin discussion of the other Roosevelt. FDR did quite a bit toward demonstrating the publicity powers of the presidency, too. Chalmers Roberts is one of America's foremost journalists, a columnist for the *Washington Post* and author of a number of books.

ROBERTS: Thank you. On Tuesday, May 18, 1937, President Roosevelt began his 367th press conference by saying,

> I am going to ask you for a very few minutes to resolve ourselves into a Committee of the Whole. Off the record, wholly off the record. I wanted to tell you a story that I think you ought to know because it does affect the press of the country. I think you will all agree on that, when you hear what I am going to read. As you know, I have always encouraged, and am entirely in favor of, absolute freedom for all news writers. That should be and will continue to be the general rule in Washington.

What FDR went on to say was this: The McClure Syndicate circulated to some 270 newspapers each week a pink sheet containing information for editors, a sort of confidential news tip sheet. This was in addition to so-called white sheets, stories intended for publication. The President then read from the latest pink sheet, to wit:

> Unchecked. A New York specialist high in the medical field is authority for the following, which is given in the strictist confidence to editors: Toward the end of last month Mr. Roosevelt was found in a coma at his desk. Medical examination disclosed the neck rash which is typical of certain disturbing symptoms. Immediate treatment of the most skilled kind was indicated, with complete privacy and detachment from official duties. Hence the trip to southern waters, with no newspapermen on board and a naval convoy which cannot be penetrated.
>
> The unusual activities of Vice President Garner are believed to be in connection with the current situation and its possible developments. "Checking has been impossible."

Roosevelt then read a second item, also from the syndicate. It concerned a private dinner in New York at which an official of American Cynamid had called the President "the paranoiac in the White House," and had gone on to declare that, "a couple of well placed bullets would be the best thing for the country, and that he for one would buy a bottle of champagne as quick as he could get it to celebrate such news."

There followed some give and take between FDR and the reporters during which the President said that the editor of the offending syndicate was one Richard Waldo. At one point a reporter asked: "Isn't that second one (the second item) actionable under law?"

To which FDR replied: "You know, that does not make any difference at all. The President of the United States does not sue for libel and the Department of Justice does not proceed for libel."

After taking up about half the press conference time, that is, about fifteen minutes I would estimate, FDR reiterated that, "It is all off the record; all strictly in the family and nothing else." And finally he said, "The Committee (of the Whole) will now recess." Whereupon the President went on to talk about and take questions on the topical issues of the day.

To the best of my knowledge all of the two hundred or so reporters—and they included a few, very few, women—observed FDR's off-the-record rule. Nothing appeared in the public prints or on radio newscasts. This was pretelevision, of course. Everybody in town naturally soon heard all about it by word of mouth. Some indignant members of the press struck at Richard Waldo, the offending editor, by having the National Press Club's board of governors call on him to show cause why he should not be expelled for insulting a fellow member—FDR. Waldo appeared—and here I quote from Oliver Clapper's 1946 book—

> and threatened each board member with libel action, declaring that their homes, savings, et cetera, would be seized if he won. The board members naturally hesitated. No formal action ever was taken but Mr. Waldo nevertheless went out of the club.

I assume he resigned.

I have cited this incident in some detail because I think it tells us a great deal, in retrospect, about the relationship between FDR and the press.

My premise today is that FDR was the best presidential communicator—to use the current term—in modern times. His honeymoon with the press lasted about two years, an extraordinary length of time. But the honeymoon did end and the normal press-president adversary relationship came into play. The approach of World War II sharpened antagonisms prior to Pearl Harbor; afterwards, both a sense of patriotism and military censorship widened the gap between press and president until his death.

In reflecting on FDR and the press, I think it is vital to go back to the beginning of his first term. I did not come to Washington until October 1933, seven months after his inauguration, but the mood I describe here was instantly evident to even a cub reporter just out of college earning fifteen dollars a week on the *Washington Post*.

You must remember that by 1933, as historian John Morton Blum has put it, " . . . the presidency had lost the stature that Theodore Roosevelt and Wilson had given it." In the Harding-Coolidge era of the 1920's, New York, not Washington, dominated the nation. The Great Depression brought demands for federal action, largely resisted by President Hoover. By the end of Hoover's term, with the depth of the Depression, relations between president and press were absymal, just about non-existent. So when FDR moved down from Albany his opportunity to change that relationship, and to do so to his advantage, was immense—and he seized that opportunity.

At his first press conference a few days after his inauguration each of the two hundred or so who crowded into the Oval Office was introduced to the President, who shook hands. Some he recognized from Albany of the campaign and he called them by their first names. You must remember that he was seated behind his desk which made it difficult for those in the back to hear, and just about impossible to see him. I know because at times I stood in the back rows, in 1933–34.

That first day FDR announced that he would divide what he wanted to say into (1) statements attributable to him but only in indirect quotation, (2) material for direct quotation which was relatively rare and usually on request of reporters to use, in quotes, some striking phrase, (3) background information that showed up in print under such euphemisms as "the President is known to think that . . . " and (4) off the record information ranging from the incident I have cited to comments on individuals or nations that often subtly colored the reporting about both.

All of this was such a switch from Hoover that at the end of that first press conference the reporters broke into applause. I don't believe that has ever happened again.

Why did they applaud? Because the reporters knew they were going to have access to news, the meat and potatoes of their profession. And because, as it turned out, that access was extensive and continuous. Despite the war, FDR, in just over twelve years in the White House, held 998 press conferences, a sea change from his predecessors and a record unmatched by his successors. They usually were held on Tuesday mornings and Friday afternoons, to give a time break to afternoon and then morning papers. As Frank Luther Mott, dean of historians of journalism, put it,

> He knew what newspapermen recognized as a good story, and he knew as well as they did how and when to 'break' it. Moreover, he was genial to the point of exuberance, and it was clear that he thoroughly enjoyed the give and take of the mass press conference.

And of course FDR had a facility of phrases: the "horse and buggy" Supreme Court of the Nine Old Men, the "garden hose" to help the allies like helping a neighbor, the shift from "Dr. New Deal" to "Dr. Win the War."

The White House was much more open to the press in those years, especially the pre-war years. In some previous administrations the press, or some of them, had been invited to one or another of the rather formal annual White House receptions along with the top bureaucrats, the military and/or the diplomats. FDR gave the press its own annual reception. I remember them well. He sat in a chair in the East Room smiling up at us as we came up to shake hands. Eleanor was at his side. There was punch and snacks and dancing in both the East Room and outside on the top of the adjoining portico to the east wing. I relish a story about George Bookman, one of the Post's White House reporters. He and his date were still enjoying one such party at two o'clock in the morning when Mrs. Roosevelt said sweetly: "Isn't it a little late for ice cream?"

FDR's sense of humor was a winner with the press. One day, when he was laid up in bed with a cold, the *Post* pulled a classic typographical error. The page one headline read: FDR IN

BED WITH COED. Hardly had that early edition reached the White House than a *Post* reporter picked up the phone to hear: "This is Frank Roosevelt. I'd like 100 copies of that first edition of the *Post*. I want to send it to all my friends." Alas, the circulation department had scurried out to recover all the papers from the corner stands and destroy them. FDR never got his 100 copies.

Roosevelt, as that veteran reporter Richard L. Strout recently put it in an interview, had charm and magnetism and an ability to think quickly. John Gunther wrote that in twenty minutes FDR's features "expressed amazement, curiosity, mock alarm, genuine interest, worry, rhetorical playing for suspense, sympathy, decision, playfulness, dignity, and surpassing charm." He knew how to answer and how to dodge. He knew how to play on particular egos and how to tell the reporters it was not they, he was sure, but their Tory bosses, the publishers, who wrote such terrible things about him and his New Deal.

But the honeymoon could not last. After all, the issues are what count with reporters. When the New Deal began to run out of steam and when FDR took on the Supreme Court some reporters grew critical, others outright hostile. Occasionally FDR would tell a particular reporter to go stand in the corner with a dunce cap for asking what he considered a silly or dumb question, but that seemed mostly to be in jest. With the coming of the bitter pre-war struggle over possible American participation in World War II some press relationships grew extremely hostile and some of this continued after Pearl Harbor. At one point FDR awarded a hypothetical Iron Cross to a reporter. It happened this way. John O'Donnell, who wrote for the *New York News* which had been bitterly isolationist, reported that the army was issuing contraceptives to the WAC's, the new women's army corps. He had gotten the story, I'm told, from Clare Luce who was no FDR admirer. Roosevelt knew it was true but he took the tack that to say so in print was unpatriotic. O'Donnell, himself, avoided Roosevelt press conferences so at the next one FDR asked Earl Godwin, one of the front row regulars known as a Roosevelt fan, to give the Iron Cross to O'Donnell. Whether a medal actually was handed to Godwin, let alone O'Donnell, I don't know—I doubt it—but the incident left a sense of bitterness against the President even among journalists who thought little of O'Donnell himself. It certainly was one of FDR's least admirable moments.

That Roosevelt had reason to dislike—yes, hate—some of the barons of the press in that pre-TV era is evident from another incident. In 1935, as the honeymoon was ending, he got hold of an international Hearst empire message from a Hearst executive to its news service, saying,

> The Chief [as William Randolph Hearst liked to be called] instructs that the phrase Soak the Successful be used in all references to the Administration's tax program instead of the phrase Soak the Thrifty hitherto used; also he wants the words Raw Deal used instead of New Deal.

James MacGregor Burns recounted that an indignant FDR wanted to make the message public but that more prudent counsel prevailed. Anti-Roosevelt publishers used to complain that FDR had hypnotized their Washington reporters with his charm and misled them with his propaganda, as Leo Rosten put it in his 1937 book on *The Washington Correspondents*.

One of the reporters who had come down from Albany with Roosevelt was Ernest K. Lindley who had written the first FDR biography. But when Lindley wrote something FDR disliked about a New York political fight, the President demanded, at a press conference, that the reporter apologize. On another occasion he denied a Lindley story that FDR had picked Secretary of State Hull to be his successor in 1940 and that he had vetoed Jim Farley because he was a Catholic. At the next press conference Roosevelt said the story was made of whole cloth but that, as the *Post* next day put it in paraphrase, he considered Lindley's to be " . . . one of the most respected columns that he considered only about twenty percent wrong, as against other columns that are eighty percent wrong." Incidentally, reporters then had no access to the White House transcript of press conferences and the tape recorder was not yet born.

When the President is an activist the press tends to play him up as an individual. Witness Kennedy and now Reagan. In FDR's case, as Reston put it in 1937,

> The Washington correspondents had propagated the impression that Franklin D. Roosevelt was a paragon of talents and a repository of supreme political skills. Events which shattered this idea released that iconoclasm which is the successor to faith.

Something akin to that has been happening in Washington this fall.

It is always easier for historians, especially in such a lovely setting as we are in today, to look back, read the now available printed record, reflect and then discern the strands of greatness or of failure in any presidency. Roosevelt's unprecedented twelve years in the White House centered on two of the most cataclysmic events of our national existence, the Great Depression and World War II. And we still argue about the economics of the former and the causes of the latter.

The press in those great events was a conveyor belt between government and public. The correspondents who crowded into those 998 press conferences were the technicians for that process. On occasion individual journalists did influence the course of history or deflect government from its course. But even such occasions were incidental to the conveyor belt function. Then, as now, the messenger—to change the metaphor—often brought unpleasant news and the recipients of the news, the public, cried out for the head of the messenger. Remember Watergate.

What was the lasting role, the historical role, of the press in the age of Roosevelt? Did it go beyond the role of the messenger, the function of the conveyor belt that applies to all administrations?

Yes, it did, and it did so just as FDR's four administrations have affected our nation for almost a half century since that first inauguration day. In time, many of the New Deal measures have been altered, watered down, strengthened, or otherwise changed. But the central point—that the federal government has basic obligations to its citizenry—remains, though it clearly has been, and today still is, under challenge. Nonetheless, I do not think we are going to see a return to the states' rights, or to the county poorhouses, of pre-FDR eras.

Those of us in the press who came of age in the FDR years could no more escape being influenced by him and his New Deal and his internationalism than could the nation as a whole. And the influence has been just as lasting. I believe that only the influence on the press of the American Revolution and of the Civil War have matched that of FDR and of his stewardship of the New Deal and his direction of the allied effort in World War II. More than one generation of newsmen and women in Washington—and indeed all across the land—have reflected that, myself included. Many were isolationists in foreign affairs and believers in states' rights, or at least in state responsibility, in domestic affairs. It is true, as many conservatives have been contending for some time now, that the press, most especially the Washington press, tends to be liberal in its outlook, probably more so than the public as a whole. And that is true not only of those remaining few of us who were here in Washington with FDR in 1933 but most of those who arrived prior to Pearl Harbor. Those who came to the Capital in, say 1939, right out of college, are today the most senior among the current crop of active journalists. Nor should we neglect the effect on a second generation of journalists who were in grade school, or not even born, during the Depression and who now can vividly recall their parents' accounts of FDR and the New Deal, just as the oldest among us still can recall tales of the venerable Civil War veterans of our own early years.

It is worth mentioning, too, that the FDR aura is still remembered by our political leaders, notably by Ronald Reagan. His obeisance to the New Deal he remembers from his youth is evident in what he calls the social "safety net." That net may be getting ragged nowadays but before FDR there was no net at all, as Reagan well remembers. Perhaps Lyndon Johnson's Great Society today is being dismantled in large degree, but FDR's New Deal at home and his internationalism abroad remains very much central to this nation, and journalists by and large reflect this.

Today it is hard to imagine a Washington press corps all crowded into the rather small Oval Office. It is hard to imagine a president who never appeared on television, for whom the radio was a rather sparingly used device to go over the heads of the antagonistic press lords to the voters, and for whom the twice weekly press conference was thus so vital a means of communication and influence. But all that was true of FDR and even to recall it is, to me, both a stimulating exercise and a refreshing reminder that this nation, the press very much included, is far better off today for Franklin D. Roosevelt having passed this way.

HARRY S. TRUMAN

THOMPSON: We turn now to FDR's successor, President Harry S. Truman.

DONOVAN: Let us begin consideration of Truman's relations with the press by listening to his own words. He had been in office about a month when I find his first reference to newspapers— "Those damned sheets." He had been in office less than a year when he discussed his relations with the press with Harold D. Smith, then the budget director. On January 31, 1946, Smith wrote in his diary:

> After a press conference, he told me that press conferences were getting rather touchy, and they tended to put him on edge. He commented that some of the questions were close to being impertinent, though he felt that the questioners did not intend them to be so. They were sometimes difficult to answer off-the-cuff because of the tendency to put a wrong interpretation on quick answers.

And quick answers were what the reporters usually got from Harry Truman. In June of 1946, President Truman received a letter from Henry A. Wallace, who was aggrieved that the press had misinterpreted what Wallace had said about the removal of troops from Iceland. The President in a "Dear Henry" letter replied on June 7, "It seems that *Life, Time* and *Fortune* magazines take particular delight in garbling anything that either you or I have to say." On March 7, 1947, Truman replied to a letter from Senator J. William Fulbright, who also complained of having been misinterpreted in the press. Truman said, "You can rest assured that I never let press comments or statements by gossip columnists affect my attitude toward my friends." Incidentally, President Truman seemed to link all columnists with gossip columnists. In a rather far-fetched comment he told Fulbright, "It is a policy of the press, of course, to create a breach or a mis-understanding between members of the same party, particularly under conditions such as exist now. I have had too much experience to allow it to affect me so don't worry about it."

Well, we'll see whether it affected him or not. Consider, for example, a letter Truman wrote on March 13, 1948, to Senator Joseph C. O'Mahoney, thanking him for the passage of legislation to restore the President's emergency fund. The President said,

> *Time* and *Life* and the scandal press, represented by Hearst and the McCormick-Patterson Axis have been spending most of their time belittling the President. The last issue of *Time* spends three or four pages telling how people of brains are kept from the White House. The Emergency Fund was used to bring brains to the White House.... There seems to be a set pattern of belittling the President and his Cabinet and of using every effort possible to prevent the Executive Branch of the Government from obtaining the information necessary on which to base decisions.

Truman wrote another letter in this vein on December 11, 1948, to Oscar R. Ewing, Federal Security Administrator, who had complained, "I didn't say what I have been quoted as saying." Truman said,

> Matt Connelly handed me the memorandum from Tris Coffin to you, and I've a very sincere notion that if there's any trouble brewing on the Hill along the lines which he states, he and his sabotage sheet are brewing it and not our friends. I want to caution you not to trust such fellows as this goofy person, because he is not a bit better than Pearson and Winchell. I've known him for a long time.

In 1948, when the national convention was approaching, the President was in a lot of political trouble with the liberals in his party, who tried to dump him, as you remember. On April 18, Truman wrote to his sister,

> Hearst, the old beast, gave a party in Los Angeles for Luella Parsons. There were about seven hundred guests and Bob Hope presided. Hearst couldn't be present. Bob Hope was explaining why. Said Hearst was not feeling well, that he was devoting all his time to building up a candidate for President (MacArthur) and that it was rumored that Hearst's candidate was flying home soon to campaign. Bob leaned over and very confidentially told the audience that the flight rumor was not true—the candidate intended to walk home.

On June 24, 1948, a presidential letter was sent to a friend in Illinois, named Martin Lewis. The subject was the influence of the *Chicago Tribune* in Illinois. "If McCormick said anything good about me," Truman observed, "I'd know it was wrong.

Sometime or other he will have to pay through the nose for all that batch of lies he has been putting out."

On May 12, 1948, the President wrote to his sister:

I've been reading a couple of books, one about the presidents and the press and another called *This Was Normalcy*. It seems that every man in the White House was tortured and bedevilled by the so-called free press. They were lied about, misrepresented and actually libelled, and they have to take it.

The old SOB who owned and edited the *St. Louis Post-Dispatch* [the sainted Pulitzer!] and *New York World* was in my opinion the meanest character assassin in the whole history of liars who have controlled the newspapers—that includes old man Hearst and Bertie McCormick.

Some day I hope a mucker will come along and dig up the facts on the distorters of news and facts.

I had thought that pictures [newsreels] and the radio would cure the news liars but they (the liars) have taken over both.

Pearson, Winchell, and local scavengers paid by such stations as WGN and WDAF make it impossible for the listeners to get the facts.

When I am finished here, maybe I'll do it myself. I'll make a bet, however, that hell has become almost untenable for the devil since Old Pulitzer, Horace Greeley, Chas. Dana and the old Copperhead, Bill Nelson [*Kansas City Star*] and William Allen White arrived.

Once, in April, 1949, Truman told David Lilienthal that, as Lilienthal recalled, " . . . he was going to even the score with Pearson" after leaving office. I never heard that he did. You know, Truman once called Drew Pearson a SOB in a speech, because of Pearson's attack on Major General Harry H. Vaughan, the President's military aide. The attack was a great one-day issue in the country, and I wish you could have seen the euphemisms that some papers felt it necessary to resort to in telling their readers what SOB meant. The general reaction to what the President said convinces you the Moral Majority is really a very old institution. The President tended to refer to Henry Luce's publications, *Time, Life*, and *Fortune*, as the "Loose" publications. In a letter of August 13, 1949, he said, "It seems to be the objective of such publications . . . along with *Look, Newsweek, Colliers*, the *Sat Evening Post*, and most of the big city newspapers to misrepresent and belittle [the President]." In a letter during the 1948 campaign—when the Truman campaign did indeed seem to be picking up in October—he wrote:

We had tremendous crowds everywhere. From six-thirty in the morning until midnight the turnout was phenomenal. The news jerks [I was one who was on the train with him] didn't know what to make of it—so they just lied about it.

Well, what do you make of that? A reporter on those campaign trains had nothing else to write but straight news. We wrote the news perfectly straight.

As far as the crowds went, there was a lot of copy about Truman's crowds. I admit that having covered only the Truman train, I supposed that Dewey was drawing the same crowds, but evidently he was not. But crowds are most misleading. I am certain that the biggest crowds that Truman ever got in the 1948 campaign were in Indiana. People were hanging from fire escapes. Yet Truman lost Indiana. The biggest crowds I remember seeing for Jack Kennedy were in Ohio, and Kennedy lost Ohio. I am told that Al Smith had tremendous crowds and lost the election. So I don't know in truth what reporters can say about the crowds, or what conclusions they can draw from crowds, other than to report them. In June, 1948, Truman wrote—and I don't have the whole text here—a letter to Walter Lippmann, couched in terms most unsuited to Lippmann's dignity. The letter, with its army latrine humor was never mailed. Truman said in it that he understood that Lippmann worked in an ivory tower but should work in a latrine. In this connection, Truman told his staff a story he had heard from Secretary of War Robert Patterson. Patterson, according to the President, said several doughboys were in an eight-hole latrine and from the one on number three hole there was a big explosive sound and the number one man said, 'Thanks for the fresh air.' The President wrote in that unmailed letter that the trouble with Lippmann was he didn't give forth with any fresh air.

After the 1948 campaign the President wrote a tart letter to Elmo Roper. Roper, you know, had ceased conducting his poll for the *New York Herald Tribune* in September of 1948, saying that the election was already over, a runaway for Dewey.

I have read with much interest, [Truman wrote,] your piece in this Morning's *Trib* headed 'A Study of Election Poll Results.'

It is interesting, but it still misses the main point. Candidates make election contests, not pole [sic] takers or press comments by paid column writers. Edited news columns and misleading headlines have some effect—not much. People in general have lost faith in the modern press and its policies.

That is a good thing, too. No one segment should be able to control public opinion. Leadership still counts. The publishers press is a very small part of our population. They have debauched the responsibility they owe to the country and the people have shown them just how they like it.

In preparing notes for his inaugural address at the start of his second term in 1949, Truman mentioned the press, although the passages never became part of the speech. Again, however, the words of the draft reveal the President's attitude. He said:

Now, I have no bitterness in my heart against anyone, not even the bitter opposition press and its henchmen, the paid columnists and managing editors and the bought and paid for commentators. Never in the history of the country did a President need the honest help and cooperation of the Congress, press and the people as I have needed them since September of 1945.

He continued, "We have the greatest republic in the world if we remember that the people elect us to do what we think is right and not what some pollster or misguided editorial writer tells us to do."

All through here you get a sense of private resentment on the part of the President. He burned about press coverage. Take, for example, a letter he wrote in mid-February, 1949, to Frank Kent, a political commentator for the *Baltimore Sun*. Truman resented Kent's attacks on his budget. The President, "I'm really surprised because I've always thought you intellectually honest. From David Lawrence, Pegler, Pearson, Winchell, I'd expect just such statements as you made—but you know that they are all liars and intellectually dishonest." I quote from a diary entry of March 26, 1949, in which Truman briefly alluded to the press. He said: "Pearson's no good. He, Fulton Lewis [Fulton Lewis was in those days, as you all remember here, a very influential radio commentator who constantly attacked the liberal Democrats] & Walter Winchell (Winchelleski) are pathological liars par excellance [sic]." Several times Truman referred in private conversations, as did Harry Vaughan, to "Winchelleski." I am not sure that was Walter Winchell's original name, and I think there's a real bias in there in calling him "Winchelleski."

In a note in the President's papers, dated March 5, 1950, Truman wrote, "People no longer in this great country can be fooled by people who write for money." I do not know what the

President thought we were going to write for. The note added that people no longer could " ... be misled by such lousy editors and managers as Hearst, McCormick, Roy Howard, Roy Roberts [*Kansas City Star*] and old man Gannett."

On June 20, 1950, Truman wrote to David Lawrence, newspaper columnist and publisher of *US News & World Report*, complaining of Lawrence's comments on the Basing Point Bill. The President said: "You should carefully read the record on Pittsburgh Plus [that was an amendment, Pittsburgh Plus]; you should read the cement case, which I am sure you haven't. Don't let the NAM write all your columns."

These are all documents from the Truman Library. In another one of these long diary records, dated September 12, 1950, Truman talks about the Scripps-Howard and the McCormick and the Hearst press and "all the rest of the traitorous and sabotage press. . . . In the meantime, in the usual Washington manner, a leak appeared in the form of an article by Tony Vaccaro saying [Louis A.] Johnson [Secretary of Defense] was to be fired. Where it came from no one can find out." The President in the first summer of the Korean War, in 1950, had really come to a climax in his difficulties with Louis Johnson, and in August of that year, an article appeared on the front page of many papers, an Associated Press piece by Ernest B. Vaccaro [we called him Tony] of the Associated Press, saying that Johnson was on his way out. Truman and all of his associates were sorely puzzled as to how that story got out. As he said, "Where it came from no one can find out." Tony Vaccaro, as did everyone in the press, knew at the time that there was terrible trouble between the President and Johnson, and that Johnson was an embarrassment to the President. Vaccaro saw Bill Boyle, the Democratic National Chairman, on the street, and he asked Bill Boyle about it. Bill said, "Tony, he's in real trouble, he's on his way out." No one else ever thought of Boyle as the source.

Here's a letter to Senator Estes Kefauver, on September 21, 1950, at a time when there was a great deal of criticism of the Truman scandals and also when Truman was in a lot of trouble with the American Medical Association over compulsory medical insurance. The AMA, as you all remember, waged an intense campaign against medical insurance, killing it in Truman's time. Truman wrote to Kefauver:

The American Medical Association and Scripps-Howard are responsible for the socialized medicine propaganda lies which have been made a whipping boy to beat the Health Program. They had similar scare words to beat the Social Security, the Securities and Exchange Act, and several other of our great legislative reforms in favor of the common everyday man.

As far as deficit financing is concerned. I've never been for deficit financing. That situation was brought about entirely by the 80th Congress and the pinheaded approach to government financing advocated by Scripps-Howard press. Of course, they have been so nasty in their editorial policy toward me that a 'half-way all right editorial' is something to write home about.

In another letter of September 24, 1950, he talked about lies. He said that lies and mud make

'news—the truth and flowers do not.' But when I read what the lousy press of the days of Washington, Jefferson, Jackson, Lincoln, Grover Cleveland, and Woodrow Wilson had to say about those men, I'm comforted, for I've had it easy by comparison.

November of 1950 was both the time of off-year elections, disappointing to Truman, and of difficulties in the Korean War. Writing to Thomas L. Stokes, a liberal columnist and a lovely man, whom Truman liked, the President said:

One of the main difficulties with which we are faced now is the campaign of the 'big lie.' There are certain chain newspapers in this country that are using a Soviet propaganda program in our political set up. I am going to spend the rest of my life in an endeavor to cause a return to truthful writing and reporting. It seems to me that when publishers pay money to men like Pearson, Winchell, Pegler, [George] Sokolsky, Trohan [Walter Trohan was the Washington Bureau Chief of the *Chicago Tribune*] and John O'Donnell [Washington Bureau Chief and columnist for the *New York Daily News*] there is something radically wrong with the moral set up of the country. A free press is a free press because it is supposed to freely publish the facts on both sides of every question. That is not done in the Hearst, McCormick and Roy Howard press. However, I am not particularly worried about their influence because I don't think they have any.

In that fall of 1950, the *Chicago Tribune* was nosing around in Kansas City about some story on the Truman family that was never published, so I don't really know what it was, but the reporter's name was Holmes. Truman wrote to a Kansas City friend that Matt Connelly had handed him a letter which his friend had written to Truman telling him about this investigation. Truman replied, "There isn't a word of truth in that

Chicago Tribune venture. You might tell the gentleman named Holmes that if he comes out with a pack of lies about Mrs. Truman or any of my family, his hide won't hold shucks when I get through with it."

Let me cite an exchange of letters in January, 1950, between Truman and Senator Brien McMahon, chairman of the Joint Congressional Committee on Atomic Energy. McMahon told the President that a piece on atomic strategy by the columnists Joseph and Stewart Alsop, who were brothers, did not come from him. Truman answered: "I don't know where the Sop Sisters got their information but evidently somebody thinks it is proper to talk to such lying scoundrels. I don't."

Incidentally, I sent Joe Alsop a copy of this in 1980, thinking he would relish being called a lying scoundrel, but he was very much hurt by it. He said, "I thought the President liked me." As a matter of fact, Joe wrote to former President Truman on March 12, 1965. That would have been during the Johnson administration. Joe, therefore, had had a chance to look at Eisenhower, Kennedy and the beginning of Johnson, and he wrote the letter, apologizing for what he called the inexperience and bad judgement which led him to underrate Truman's leadership while in office. In retrospect, Alsop said, "the Truman years seemed to him a truly heroic period." Over the years, you know we all think a former president is better after we've seen the one currently in office. And I must say that Nixon has brought every one else way up—even Franklin Pierce. Truman acknowledged Alsop's letter very graciously.

Truman's comments, to which I have alluded today, create a strong impression of his attitude toward the press. Here is a memorandum which I think is a self-explanatory one from the President to J. Howard McGrath, the Attorney General. Truman said:

> In the main editorial in the February thirteenth issue of the *Chicago Daily Tribune* they had the nerve to make the statement that Truman is a crook, which I think is libel and criminal libel at that. I wish you would get copies of that editorial, read it carefully, and then proceed with whatever action is necessary to get the right result. Not only is it a libel to myself, but it brings Vaughan and Mrs. Truman into the picture.

Nothing ever came of this; no suit was ever brought by the President.

Here is a case of the President's using a little muscle in a memorandum for the secretary of the army, on March 24, 1951:

> I have learned that Philip Cranden Woodyatt, who is employed in your office, secured his employment thru Drew Pearson.
>
> I am attaching a paper which indicates that Woodyatt, while a resident of Fresno, California, was in close association with Mr. Pearson's son-in-law, George Arnold (son of Thurman Arnold) a Los Angeles attorney, and was of considerable help to Mr. Pearson in his legal fight with Attorney General Howser.
>
> This gentleman may be one of the leaks to Pearson in the Defense Department. I wish you would look into it.

The *New Republic*, in 1951, wrote an editorial on the Truman scandals, likening the Truman administration to the Harding administration. Jonathan Daniels, who had been Franklin D. Roosevelt's press secretary and briefly Truman's, sent Truman a copy of it. The President wrote back, saying, among other things:

> That *New Republic* article was the usual result of 'professional liberal thinking.' I have never found a professional liberal yet who really knew the score—it takes practical men, as Theodore Roosevelt said, to run the government but the practical men must be honest to begin with, and I think most of them are.

In a letter to Senator William Benton on August 15, 1951, Truman was highly critical.

> There is [he said] a concerted effort on the part of the wire services, Associated Press and the United Press to discredit whatever the administration forces try to do. If you will analyze the manner in which they handled McCarthy and the manner in which they handle people who are members of the Administration you will see what I mean.

The President, and he was not alone in this, was very angry at the press for making a big story about everything Senator Joseph R. McCarthy said. There is no question but what it was a very difficult time for the American press. The press was not prepared for McCarthy any more than Truman was prepared, and he wasn't prepared at all, and didn't know how to handle him. Truman was, with some justification, resentful of the play McCarthy was getting in the news media.

Truman's letter to Benton continued:

> When the St. Louis Post Dispatch made an unfounded attack on Bill Boyle [it was not unfounded] and got nowhere with it they blew it up sky high on the wire services and gave it to every paper in the country. When the Milwaukee Journal and the Capitol Times state the facts on

McCarthy and his income tax escapades the wire services inform the Milwaukee Journal and the Capitol Times that they must make an investigation to be sure of the facts, but they didn't wait to be sure of the facts with regard to Mr. Boyle, as he happened to be a Democrat and head of the Democratic National Committee.

You will find if you study the lines followed by these press people, that they are just as guilty of sabotaging the news as Pravda and Izvestia in Russia. Of course they're not going to be able to get away with it anymore than they did in nineteen hundred and forty-eight, and, before this thing is ended you and I are going to teach them a lesson.

The President wrote a letter on August 8, 1951 saying, "Never a day passes that some scalawag or some high-class publication doesn't take a swipe at my character and integrity and ancestry." He usually referred to the *Washington News*, then a Scripps-Howard paper, as the "snotty little *News*." Another paper at the time was the Washington *Times Herald*, and the President wrote on January 8, 1952,

The sabotage sheet, the *Washington Times Herald* is Bertie McCormick's outlet in the capital city. His *Chicago Tribune* and the *New York Daily News*, are his lie outlets in those two great cities. Roy Howard's chain and the Knight layout are Hearst imitators, but not quite up to the dirtiest Hearst technique. But they are coming along. . . .

In February 1952, one of the big stories was whether the President was going to run for re-election. It was therefore a frequent subject in press conferences. Truman wrote a letter February 12, 1952, saying that he was going to keep the secret to himself until he was ready to announce it. "In that way," he noted, "I can nail the lies of the sabotage press and the lying air commentators and the columnists whose business it is to prostitute the minds of the voters."

In a grumpy mood on December 6, 1952, toward the end of his term, he noted in his diary that the press was infested with some "lice" and snapped,

To hell with them. When history is written they will be the sons-of-bitches—not I.

Look at old Medill, Horace Greely *et. al.* in Lincoln's time. Biddle in Jackson's and old man Pulitzer in Cleveland's.

It isn't Jackson's, Lincoln, and Cleveland who were wrong!

What does one say about this? I have spent a lot of my life among politicians. I never met one that could really take the press. I never met one who could understand, or was willing to see the press's side of the problem, though granted there is much to criticize in the press. I always have had the feeling—I haven't written it, because I can't prove it—but I think that Truman did what a lot of people do. After a long day he went home and downed a few bourbons, then he wrote this fiery stuff about the press. The next day all was calm again. My first close experience with a politician was with New York's Mayor Fiorello LaGuardia. I covered him for the *Herald Tribune* and that's where I really came to understand politics and the press. LaGuardia was made by the New York press; he would have been nothing without it. He opposed Tammony Hall. Most of the papers, therefore, supported him in a huge way, and yet he carried on about the press. I saw LaGuardia grab a reporter's notes and tear them up. I remember one occasion early in the war when he was giving awards to the Sanitation Department and he had all these street cleaners lined up in front of city hall, with their carts and their brooms, in military formation. Over a loudspeaker that carried his voice all the way to the *World-Telegram* building, he said to these gentlemen, "I'm glad"—this was right after Pearl Harbor—"there's not a Jap-lover in this group." He said, "I'm *glad* there isn't a Jap-lover like Roy Howard! And what do you think Roy Howard did? He went over and he bowed down before the Mikado."

I know for a fact that Dwight D. Eisenhower, who had the kind of press that most presidents dare not even dream of, was absolutely fuming that he couldn't get this story across, that the press wasn't telling the story. So it goes on. I don't regard Truman's outbursts as unique. Truman stood in the tradition of the old Middle-Western Progressives. He spoke their idiom. He fought the railroads; in fact, he conducted a big investigation of the railroads in the Senate. The banks. High rates. He fought the "interests." The language was almost of the Teddy Roosevelt era, and in Truman's view, the Big Press were the interests. Furthermore, Scripps-Howard and McCormick and Hearst made a big game of going after Truman. There was no attempt on their part, really, to treat him in a balanced sort of way.

To those big papers, which were very powerful chains, Truman was the enemy. Truman knew it and responded accordingly. We don't have anything comparable today that I'm aware of though I'm not a reader of the *New York Post*. The press I am familiar with in recent years does not at all behave like Scripps-Howard and Hearst and McCormick in Truman's days. The *Chicago Tribune* today is nothing like it was. When Truman went to Los Angeles in 1948, he received an honorary degree and delivered the commencement address in the 100,000-seat stadium at the University of California at Berkeley. There were 60,000 people in the audience. The *Chicago Tribune* reported that there were 40,000 empty seats. That's the kind of thing that angered Truman.

A president's press relations are very largely influenced by the atmosphere of his time. Eisenhower, for example, had a relatively very easy time with the press, but the Eisenhower period was, in comparison with some others, a very tranquil period. Truman was in office during a very, very bitter time in this country, politically. Let me just run down a little bit of the kind of thing that kept the kettle boiling for him. Right after the war, right after he became President, we went through the greatest wave of strikes this country has ever seen, and there was tremendous controversy over the whole business of conversion from a wartime to a peacetime economy. Civil rights really came to a head in the Truman period, spurred by the return of black southern soldiers to their homes. The civil rights issue was extremely difficult for Truman. The firing of Henry Wallace and the onset of the Cold War, Truman's battles with John L. Lewis, troubles with the Republican 80th Congress roiled the first term. Truman had to battle Democratic liberals who tried to dump him in 1948 in favor of Eisenhower.

The second term was hell for Truman. The Republicans were absolutely bitter about what happened to them in 1948; they were implacably hostile to Truman. The Hiss case came along, coloring politics in this country for years. China fell to the Communists. McCarthy almost tore the country from its moorings. War erupted in Korea. Truman was plunged into a political crisis over the relief of General MacArthur and into a constitutional crisis over the seizure of the strike-threatened steel industry. The administration was shaken by a series of scandals. So President Truman was President in a time of great political bitterness and change in this country. This was reflected in his relations with the press and the kinds of questions he was asked. Ronald Reagan has held five press conferences at this point in his administration. President Truman had fifty. Altogether he had, I think, 347 press conferences. He inherited a tradition, set by Roosevelt, of weekly press conferences and lived up to it. I would never have said this as a reporter, but I think there were times when President Truman only made trouble for himself by not cancelling press conferences because of difficult situations.

What is to me the classic case was President Truman's press conference of November 30, 1950. It was a terrible time in this country. The Chinese had come into the war and were rolling our armed forces back down the Korean peninsula. The government didn't know but what we were heading for war with China and possibly with the Soviet Union. Everything was in flux. That's the worst possible time for a president to have a press conference, but Truman went ahead on that day, regardless. I'll read a little bit of it to you. In this terrible atmosphere the President got up and announced that the forces of the United Nations had no intention of abandoning Korea. As a matter of fact our military had not yet decided whether we could hold Korea indefinitely. The President then announced what was going to happen. He talked about the build-up of military strength; he was going to ask Congress for 10 billion dollars. "The request," he said, "will include a substantial amount for the Atomic Energy Commission, in addition to large amounts for the Army, Navy and Air Force." This mention of the Atomic Energy Commission triggered a thought among the reporters, inevitably. One reporter asked if it was up to the United Nations whether Manchuria would be attacked. Truman replied that it was. Then came the question: "In other words, if the United Nations Resolution should authorize General MacArthur to go further than he has, he will . . . " Interruption. Truman said, "We will take whatever steps are necessary to meet the military situation just as we always have." Jack Doherty of the *New York Daily News* asked, "Will that include the atomic bomb?" Previously under similar circumstances, President Truman had said no, absolutely not, but this time he said, in reply to Doherty, "That includes every weapon that we have." Paul R. Leach of the *Chicago Daily News* then asked, "Does that mean that there is active consideration of the use of the atomic bomb?" Truman might have ended the discussion then and there, if he had replied, that at his level of the government no new consideration was being given to using the bomb, which would have been, on all evidence, true. Instead he answered, keeping this going:

> There has always been active consideration of its use. I don't want to see it used. It is a terrible weapon, and it should not be used on innocent men, women, and children who have nothing whatever to do with this military aggression. That happens when it is used.

Just at that point, when it seemed that the atomic bomb question had been ended by Truman's saying he did not want to use the bomb, Merriman Smith of the United Press asked for a recapitulation of what the President had said on the atomic bomb. Although this led to mischief, it was a fair enough request for a wire service reporter who wanted to be certain that out of the rapid discussion he was clear as to just what the President had meant on a sensitive subject. In effect, giving Truman an opportunity to restate the case unmistakably, Smith asked, "Did we understand you clearly that the use of the atomic bomb is under active consideration?" This question, in the midst of one of the greatest crises since Pearl Harbor. "Always has been," Truman replied. "It is one of our weapons." "Does that mean, Mr. President," asked Robert G. Nixon of the old International News Service, "use against military objectives or civilians?" Whether he was aware that the reporters were now developing a big story, Truman responded, "It is a matter that the military people will have to decide. I'm not a military authority that passes on those things." Then: "Mr. President, you say this depends on the United Nations action. Does that mean that we wouldn't use the atomic bomb except on United Nations authorization?" "No, it doesn't mean that at all," Truman answered. "The action against Communist China depends on the action of the United Nations. The military commander in the field will have charge of the use of weapons as he always has."

Truman failed to note that the Atomic Energy Act of 1946 provides that only the President may order the use of atomic weapons. Reporters who knew, or should have known, of this provision, bolted for the telephones at the end of the conference with the uppermost impression that Truman had indicated that MacArthur might give the order. Truman's language had been a perfect prescription for causing confusion among over-excited reporters working in a hasty, competitive situation. Given the mindless competition for headline news then prevailing among three wire services at the White House, the consequences were inevitable. Within minutes the United Press bulletin said, "President Truman said today that the United States has under consideration use of the atomic bomb in connection with the war in Korea." A similar Associated Press lead reported further down in the story that Truman had said that the decision on whether to drop atomic bombs was one for the commander in the field.

Shortly after this, the White House issued a statement saying that Truman's words had not changed the strategic situation in any way and that the President had not authorized the use of nuclear weapons. The news from the press conference travelled so fast, however, that huge headlines based on the wire services' stories blossomed around the country and around the world. It was a tremendous shock at the United Nations, especially among the non-white nations. Mrs. Franklin D. Roosevelt, a member of the American delegation, immediately sent this report to George C. Marshall, secretary of state:

> The people of the whole Asiatic continent would never understand why the American people had decided to use the bomb against them. They would regard it as an action of the white race against the colored races. They would never forget that the atomic bomb was used first against the Japanese and later against the Chinese, but never against any white people. This fact would have a disastrous effect upon the relations of the United States with the rest of the world for years to come.

From Paris to New Delhi, headlines blazed. In Finland they conveyed the notion that Truman already had given MacArthur the fateful order. In Rome, *Il Momento* reported that the bombers were ready to take off at one hour's notice. The headline in a paper from Poland that I can't pronounce was: "Atomic Bombs Plans of Truman, Acheson & Co." *Avanti*, a socialist newspaper in Italy, carried a headline: "Washington Disregarded United Nations." The *Times of India* ran an editorial under the heading "No No No." The sharpest reaction, as you all remember, occurred in London. Parliament was in session, and Truman's words created an upheaval. In the face of this pressure, Prime Minister Clement R. Attlee called the President and said he must come and talk to him, and that was the source of the famous Attlee-Truman conference in Washington in December 1950. So this was a case, I think, of one press conference too many.

There have been people who have speculated that Truman raised fear of the atomic bomb deliberately to cause China to halt the attack. I toyed with that idea for a long time but gave it up. Truman wrote a couple of notes to friends afterwards, dismayed by the sensation. He said he had had no ulterior intent in doing this; he was just answering questions. The answers were certainly clumsy and impulsive.

I think those of us here who were around in those years relished Truman press conferences. They were full of zip, full of humor, full of news, though often very light on sustenance. Truman did not use the press conference well enough to educate people. Truman was anything but an expert on foreign affairs and he wisely left work on foreign policy to others, but on domestic issues he had come to office well-grounded and could have used press conferences better. He had been on the Senate Appropriations Committee, and the Senate Military Affairs Committee. In fact, his budget press conferences in the White House *were* a real education. Truman understood government, he understood budgets, he understood the military structure. But his press conferences were staccato. At one of those press conferences he complained, in a rather nice way, about press reports referring to him as being "cocky." Truman said, as I recall his words, "I am not cocky, and I wish you wouldn't say I'm cocky." He was right about that. I never thought Truman as being cocky, because "cocky" doesn't go well with humility, and I think Truman was essentially a humble man. But when Truman was under attack, his tendency was to fight back; he was a counterpuncher. And I think you see a lot of that in his press conferences.

Any president's personal relationships with the press have their roots in times before he came to the White House. Truman grew up in Missouri; he had become part of the Prendergast machine. The *Post-Dispatch* and the *Kansas City Star*, the big papers in Missouri, fought tooth and nail, and I think with justification, against the corrupt machine out there, against the Prendergast machine. Truman grew up seeing the big papers attack him and his organization. They opposed him, being a Prendergast man, in all his elections. Many large newspapers around the country opposed the New Deal, which was the matrix of Truman's policies in the White House. He saw the press as hostile.

Most of the reporters liked him. On the whole, I don't think Truman handled press conferences very well. He did not create the image of himself that he might have. The idea that Truman was a little man was fostered by a lot of this snippiness in his answers. But I'll say, on the other hand, he was honest; there was no managed news under his presidency. I do not remember having heard Truman accused of lying or misleading. However, he had no philosophy of a press organization. Charles G. Ross was a charming, well-grounded, well-thought-of Washington correspondent, but he was not a particularly creative press secretary. He didn't try to build Truman up where he might have; he didn't try to coordinate public information. He was a weary man; he was too old for the job; he took it reluctantly. We all came to see Charlie's failures mostly in the light of James C. Hagerty, who came along after him as Eisenhower's press secretary.

SCHERER: What impressed me about Truman was this fencing quality. He seemed to enjoy fencing with the press. But I don't know any president that had to have so many post-news conference corrections.

DONOVAN: Well, I just mentioned one.

SCHERER: It seemed to me that happened on a fairly regular basis, didn't it?

DONOVAN: Well, I remember only two of any moment. He was sounding off one time about how we stood up to the Soviet Union and he said he had sent Joe Stalin an ultimatum to get out of Azerbaijan in Iran in 1946. That caused a great to-do about Truman's having sent an ultimatum to Stalin and of course that was wrong. Later the White House had to issue the statement just referred to on the atomic bomb. Those were the two big ones, the atomic bomb and Azerbaijan. Maybe there were others but I can't remember.

SCHERER: There was a lot of camaraderie at places like Key West.

DONOVAN: But there wasn't, though.

SCHERER: A little superficial, but ...

DONOVAN: Yes, superficial. I knew Eisenhower far better than I knew Truman. I was at his stag dinners; he also gave dinners for us and he talked to us on his vacations. I never had that kind of association with Truman. I think maybe such socializing existed to some extent when he first became President and some of the reporters he knew from Senate days were invited to play with him. But this camaraderie did not last long.

Truman's press relations became very formal. You couldn't dream of asking for an interview with President Truman; and it's too bad, because Truman, one on one, was very good.

JUERGENS: There was one with Arthur Krock.

DONOVAN: Arthur Krock had one interview at a party, or as a result of having met Truman at a party. Truman knew a lot, he had a philosophy about government. Almost more than any president I've known he wanted to do what was right. He really had a feeling for common people. But I think that would have come through more clearly if he could have talked to reporters individually or in small groups the way Jack Kennedy did. There was scant television in Truman's time. What television there was was formal, and Truman was very poor on it. He had those big thick glasses, and his performance was just a matter of reading a prepared speech. He used television not at all, except . . .

SCHERER: Except the TV trip through the White House.

DONOVAN: Yes, that was the best thing he ever did.

THOMPSON: What about radio? Did you feel he was effective with radio in reaching the people?

DONOVAN: No. I did not. I thought he was awfully dull on the radio. Truman had a sing-song presentation. Truman was at his best as a whistle-stop campaigner, when he was just talking to other people. Truman was not a good formal speaker. Truman was not a good communicator. I don't think that in his prepared speeches he was a persuasive man. The way I look at President Truman is to remember that he was a former Democratic senator and that the Democratic Party was still very strong. The Democratic Party pulled him through in 1948. President Truman put his chips on the power of the Democratic Party in that campaign. His speeches played to the continuing New Deal sentiment.

JONES: One of the most interesting parts of your presentation for me was the Alsop anecdote, which I think raises a very important issue that I see as something I hope you will return to later. That is that Truman got better with Alsop's age. Does the press naturally create an image that has to be corrected later by themselves as historians? And if so, what does that say? Is there a problem of balance, a problem of the very historical perspective which you suggested is terribly important in measuring presidents in regard to their press relations? Finally, if all this is so, how does that compare with the press in other free systems? It seems to me that that touches on a number of very important matters as regards press relations at any one time, as well as press relations as a source of understanding presidents later.

DONOVAN: That is an awful big order, but I'll answer the first part of your question in any case. I've had two experiences of going through the records of presidents. I had that unusual experience in 1955–56 of having a large volume of Eisenhower's papers available to me for a book while he was still in office in his first term. Now I've just spent over ten years going through the historical record of the Truman administration. I'm prepared to argue against all the sassy remarks that you were reading from others. The American press informs the people very well of what's going on in Washington. Not perfectly, but very well. There are few surprises. I've been through these records now in masses, and we really knew and reported what was happening. There's a lot of stuff like who did Eleanor Roosevelt like and what girls Jack Kennedy was with, and so forth, that comes out, but I don't find as time goes on great new revelations of what happened. There arise differences in interpretation, of course, but the people are well informed by the press on what actually happens in Washington.

THOMPSON: Is it the adversary tone then?

DONOVAN: The tone. And of course, it doesn't mean that they are properly informed every day. The press has to write before it knows things, but then in time the picture comes into focus.

JUERGENS: I'm interested in what you say. You've heard the old line that all you Washington correspondents belong to the same race (by and large), you're all white, you're all middle to upper middle class whites, you're resident in that same community, to a certain extent you feed upon each other. You've heard all this. It's not as if the news is an objective reality; the news is what you folks define the news to be, and that's what gets written about. When you say, well, we do a good job, perhaps you are doing a good job from a particular perspective, and there would also be other people who could say, no, you're doing a terrible job because there are things that are happening in this country that you're barely writing about.

DONOVAN: Well, I was really speaking about the field of government policy.

KILPATRICK: It's in the field of government policy, it seems to me, that a serious person can determine what that policy is by reading newspapers and magazines. I think that the presidents always are annoyed terribly by some of these small things. What did Mrs. Truman wear yesterday? And that just sends them right up the wall. Should Nixon have a prayer service in the White House? That was a big issue for a while. I think the press always overemphasizes things of that sort, and I think that's why Wilson and all the rest of them became so bitter toward the press. And I do think that the Hearst press and the McCormick press in those earlier days were doing many things that are not being done today in really scandalous reporting and building up things and character attacks.

DWIGHT D. EISENHOWER

THOMPSON: Perhaps we should turn now to President Truman's successor, President Eisenhower.

SCHERER: I'll give you a brief rundown on Eisenhower for the sake of continuity. A number of us here covered him and most of this is fairly recent and fairly well-known. Eisenhower, at least in my view, was no great devotee of the presidential press conference, but he did them regularly and he almost always made news. His first one was on the 17th of February, 1953. I'd like to tell you how he began it and how he ended it, just for flavor. He said,

> First of all, ladies and gentlemen, let me assure you that I welcome this opportunity to meet with representatives of the radio and press, many of them old friends of mine, and to continue the kind of relationship that I have had in the past with them. I look forward to many of these meetings during the ensuing four years. Now one of the topics that made an interesting subject for speculation during the past few months was the thought that I would develop a great deal of antagonism for the press.

The word had gotten about that he might not hold news conferences at all or that he would hold them irregularly, or he would hold them in a kind of imperious way. I think he was told by a lot of people, notably Jim Hagerty, that he had to do it in the old way and do it regularly; and indeed he enlarged the press conference as an institution. He went on to say,

> I wouldn't know why there was this feeling that I would develop a great deal of antagonism. I feel that no individual has been treated more fairly and squarely in the past years now that I have been dealing with them, than I have by the press. Through the war years and ever since I have found nothing but a desire to dig at the truth, so far as I was concerned, and be open-handed and forthright about it. That is the kind of relationship I hope we can continue. . . . [and I have to say that he more or less did.]
> Now, of course, you know we can talk here all day. There are a lot of things in a big country such as ours and the kind of world that we are

living in that make interesting subjects for conversation. My next appointment is in my office at 11:00 [here he was setting a half-hour time period]. This morning I have chosen four subjects that I think are of immediate interest both in the domestic scene and in the international scene that can stand a little bit of discussion. Thereafter we will use such time as you might want to ask questions on these subjects, and then if there is a little time left, why, we can extend it even wider and see if there are other questions into which you might like to inquire.

Then he went on to talk about these four subjects: the first was farm prices, the second was secret agreements, the third was price controls, and the fourth was taxes. He then threw it open to the usual give-and-take; few questions went back to the four subjects he'd outlined. He wound up without the traditional thank-you from Merriman Smith; apparently he wasn't familiar with that part of the routine. He talked about the people that he'd chosen in his administration. He said, "I've tried to pick people on character and I think they have character. I think they're going to do a grand job for the United States of America." He closed this way, "And with that little bit of [he called it] political speech, with that, for the morning, goodbye, I'll see you again." That was how the first one ended.

He held them quite regularly; I think he probably averaged two or three a month over the time he was in office. They were usually at 10:30 on Wednesdays in the Indian Treaty Room where Truman had moved the news conference to make room for more reporters and to institute more decorum. Occasionally he would hold one at four o'clock. He prepared for news conferences by sitting down with News Secretary Hagerty, and, on occasion, selected cabinet officials. Hagerty would meet with a few of the press regulars before the news conference and tell them what was on the President's mind and they—I sometimes went to these—would say what was on our minds, so Hagerty generally had some idea of what was going to come up so he could brief Eisenhower. Ike and Hagerty took the news conference into several new dimensions which made it a larger and more meaningful institution. For one thing, they authorized the use of a transcript. Reporters were allowed to hire an outside transcript service to come in and set up transcribing machines and then issue an authorized transcript of the news conference, so therefore you read Eisenhower in the *New York Times* and other papers the next day in direct quotes. This, of course, made the reporting of the press conference much more vivid. He was the first president who went from indirect discourse to direct quotes. Another innovation was the use of radio recordings. Truman's news conferences were recorded, but only rarely was an excerpt given out and that was generated by the fact that somebody would ask, "Mr. Truman, may we have that in direct quotes?" He would use a particularly vivid phrase and he would say, "Yes, you may," and then you could get a little bit of recording for use on the radio news in those days.

So from the beginning, Eisenhower news conferences were in direct quotes; they were heard on the radio. Hagerty reserved the right to edit them: you couldn't go on the air with the tape of the news conference until Hagerty had said O.K. But, finally it became routine and he just kind of waved his hand as if to say, you can have it all. Eisenhower never went for either live radio or television because Hagerty would explain that there was the fear that he would misspeak. He rarely did misspeak, but they never wanted to take that chance. After a couple of years, they did allow television to make its way into the presidential news conference by way of the television film cameras. They weren't live television cameras, they weren't even television cameras, they were film cameras, which of course could be used for television. That was begun, I think, after about three years. There were a row of sixteen cameras and newsreel cameras in the back of the room. This was greatly fought, at least initially, by the old-timers who felt that it would make a show of things, make prima donnas out of reporters and would have various other deleterious effects—few of which ever happened.

So from then on, you not only heard Eisenhower on the radio news shows, you saw him that evening on the television news, which of course in those days were black and white and ran only for fifteen minutes. I remember the first time that NBC did him in color—David Brinkley took the film under his arm, he was handed it by the camera man and went out to the airport and raced to Chicago and they developed it there and the President was seen that night on color television. That's when General Sarnoff was trying very hard to sell color. So that was the third innovation.

Eisenhower also experimented with other ways of coverage.

He had various evening television specials, coached by Bob Montgomery. He sat down with various cabinet members. He had one with Dulles and Benson and one with various others. These were, I guess you would say, a middling success. He also had still another form of press relations. He would sit down with a selected group of reporters, generally the regulars, that is the 15 or so who made trips with him and were considered by Hagerty to belong to the regulars—*New York Times, New York Herald Tribune, New York News, Baltimore Sun, Washington Post* and *Star, Time, Newsweek, NBC, CBS, ABC, Chicago Tribune*—that was about it. We would come to the White House for an evening and have dinner with Eisenhower, seated around the big table. He would hold forth in a very unrestrained kind of way. Then we would have drinks and he would sit next to the piano and hold forth at further length. Then we would all go to a hotel room afterward and try to recapitulate what he had said. There was generally a deadline of a day or two—and the first time this happened, it was an absolute bombshell because nobody in Washington knew where this stuff was coming from. It suddenly appeared on the wire about two o'clock in the afternoon. He did this a number of times. These were good sounding boards for him, and he was wonderfully cordial at these occasions.

DONOVAN: That's the kind of thing Truman never did, and would have done well.

SCHERER: He would have done well. I think Ike was probably put up to these by Hagerty. For whatever reasons, he did them and he did them very well, and he got a lot of things on the record that you couldn't do in the normal give and take of a news conference. I thought his news conferences were pretty good. He frequently made news—there were as many as five stories in the *New York Times* and perhaps the *Washington Post* next morning, depending on how they wanted to break it up into various subjects. He allowed his emotions to show through, and occasionally he would get angry.

I remember the time he was asked by Bill McGaffin whether he had acquired a new helicopter so he could get to Burning Tree for golf a little quicker than before. He absolutely blew a gasket—his face was about four different colors. And there was another time when CBS had done an exclusive interview with Khrushchev. They were very proud of it, and their representative, Charles Von Fremd, got up and asked him what he thought of it, and it turned out he didn't like it at all. We told the CBS man afterwards he should have quit while he was behind.

As for press relations in general, Eisenhower did not hand out any exclusives, but various reporters were able to get exclusives by way of digging. He preferred certain newspapers to other newspapers—he particularly liked the *Herald Tribune* at which his very good friend Bill Robinson was general manager. He always got a good ride from *Time* and *Life*, he was very close to Luce and Mrs. Luce. At some point he stopped reading the *Washington Post*, or at least I had that impression. Because one morning the *Washington Post*, I think it was a Wednesday, had a piece on its front page saying that his daughter-in-law's father, Barbara Eisenhower's father, was thinking of running for governor of Florida. I got up and asked him the question—what was his name, Colonel So-and-So; Colonel Thompson, was it? I've forgotten—but I said that the Colonel was apparently going to take a leaf from him and follow a political career. I said to him I was curious as an old pol himself whether he'd have any advice to offer his daughter-in-law's father. He said, "Well, Mamie reads the kind of paper in which this news appeared." That was a clue to me that he hadn't read the *Washington Post*, or wasn't reading it. He went on to say whatever it was he said about it.

He liked some reporters better than others, but his relations with the press, I would have to say, were always rather formal except on occasions when he'd have us in or we'd give him a birthday party, in which case he could be enormously warm and very engaging. I don't know that he complained about the press, the way Mr. Truman seemed to, in nocturnal scribblings. He was asked what he thought of news conferences as such several times, and his general answer was that it went with the territory; it was part of being President, and he may not have enjoyed them, but he did them as a duty and he did them fairly well.

Occasionally, I think he was unhappy about the fact that we had to traipse along to the golf course. I think he resented us following every stroke. On one occasion when he was on vacation he got very, very frosty and didn't speak to us collectively for a couple of days. He was fishing up in Colorado, down in a trout stream with his friend Axel Neilsen and a couple of others. And we were all up above. Hagerty would always get rid of us by allowing us to photograph his first session down in Augusta on the golf course or his first fishing session—of course the photographers always clamored for it. We stood up on the bank, and I think the limit was twelve, and he fished about sixteen or eighteen. The *New York Times* the next morning had a picture of him fishing with a headline "Ike Goes Over the Limit." He glowered the next morning at the press room at Lowry Field where we were all staying. He was really frosty.

DONOVAN: But furthermore, the *New York Times* headline about Ike's overcatching his legal limit of fish came just a day or two after a speech Ike had given on moral probity.

SCHERER: Well, their story was, of course, he went over the limit but he threw them back. Didn't you see him throw them back? By that time we were shooed out of there, I suppose. So there were these occasional little contretemps, but by and large I would have to say his relations with the press were fairly normal, fairly serene. He didn't allow a lot of news conferences to build up, by which I mean he didn't go long periods without holding them, so that large pressures would build up, the sort of problem that Nixon had.

There was always a lot of talk and kidding about his tangled syntax, but if you sat in the room listening to him, you knew what he meant to say. I used to have to go on the air immediately on coming out of a press conference at eleven o'clock on live radio, and I never had any problem saying what I thought he meant to say. I think he was fair with the press; he was frustrated by not being able to get his story out as well as he might have.

I want to say something about Hagerty—Hagerty was a superb technician; he took great care of the wants and feeding of the press. Before you made a trip, Hagerty would spend hours standing at his desk giving you every detail of where you were going to go, and where the telephones would be, and where the wire links would be, and how you would broadcast. He took great pains to do all this, and in detail. We made this 19-day fourteen country trip in 1959, which was laid out in wonderful detail. Hagerty had gone over the ground ahead of him. Hagerty, I think, served him very well in that technical sense. Hagerty was not always terribly articulate or intellectually brilliant, but he was a good press secretary. He was loyal and if you went wrong on something, he was pretty good about setting you straight.

So I would say that, in sum, Eisenhower's contributions were the fact that he introduced the direct quote; he brought in radio; he edged into the television era; held regular news conferences; and wound up in 1960 on as good terms with the press as he had started out in 1953. He had a farewell party to which he invited us all and it was a very warm and wonderful occasion. I'll stop there.

JUERGENS: I have a question about these dinners he invited you to. Did he know you by name at these dinner sessions?

SCHERER: Yes, by first names.

JUERGENS: One gets the impression that sometimes he didn't know who a face belonged to.

DONOVAN: I've heard that before; he knew who reporters were.

JUERGENS: Was it like a press conference, only sitting around a table?

SCHERER: It was like a bull session. We'd ask him questions and he'd go on. It was a bull session, but he was fairly frank and everybody had a drink or two.

KILPATRICK: But these were not on the record; they were just background.

SCHERER: They were background. They would burst on the record afterwards, depending on what sort of release time Hagerty had put on them. Of course, the non-regulars didn't like it because they weren't invited. He didn't do it too often, but I would guess there were several occasions.

DONOVAN: These famous Ike stag dinners. I was invited to one and they were pretty much the same thing. These businessmen would ask him questions. Some would criticize; some he answered. The head of Dart Drug Company one time started to attack Roosevelt when I was there, and Eisenhower stepped in and gave a different point of view. He said that the Roosevelt name was a great thing for America; Roosevelt was a great name to America during the war. He said, in so many words, "I don't think you ought to downplay Roosevelt and what he did for this country." The head of Dart Drug was taken aback by this rebuke; I'm sure he thought he was getting into Ike's good graces by attacking Roosevelt!

SCHERER: There were two kinds of dinners; one would have tycoons and occasional reporters; in the dinners that I talked about, he had only reporters, about fifteen of us. He also used those to float political prospects—at one of them he had Bob Anderson. He had great respect for Anderson, and he had Anderson sit at the middle of the table—we didn't know why, but we all decided afterward that he wanted us to be impressed with Anderson as a presidential possibility. I thought that was rather naive of him.

DONOVAN: At that stag dinner I heard him give one of the best expositions of why we should recognize Red China that I have ever heard, but publicly he would never mention a thing like that, and indeed would have opposed it.

LATIMER: This is inspired by Ike's syntax reference and I do not mean to demean any of the press participants in his press conferences or any others. But the question is, was the syntax of some of the questions any better than the syntax of Eisenhower's answers?

DONOVAN: Shorter.

SCHERER: But probably no better.

LATIMER: Now that was prompted by somebody's column recently quoting some of the questions that meander around. I have been guilty of asking meandering questions like that myself. But I just wondered, is the standard of press conference questions what it should be?

SCHERER: No, it isn't; it skips around, it's helter skelter. That's quite another problem. I think Eisenhower tried to direct the occasion in his first news conference by setting out four subjects and saying he wanted to answer questions on those, but nobody paid any attention to him. The same thing happens now. The President may start out with a fairly interesting subject but the first question is invariably something else. Everybody comes with his favorite question, and the business of how you follow up has never been broadly resolved.

JUERGENS: Would you say that the press treated Eisenhower with kid gloves more than they've treated other presidents? When things came up, did the press move on them?

DONOVAN: In part, there wasn't the opportunity.

SCHERER: You didn't have constant television exposure as you have now; you have three network correspondents out on the White House lawn every night. That was very hard to do in those days. I was a White House correspondent, and you couldn't do it from the White House, technically, without bringing in a mobile unit and stringing miles of cable. You did it only on very great occasions when there was a crisis. Now it's a matter of course, and things get much more currency.

SCHERER: Another factor in the whole Eisenhower period is the rather placid relationship—although I have to say he was the general and we were the privates, except on social occasions, we were treated rather coolly—and that it was a tranquil period, as we've said before. With the exception of Little Rock and—

DONOVAN: McCarthy-Army—

SCHERER: McCarthy-Army and Sherman Adams and—

BLACKFORD: And that week when Hungary and the Middle East blew up at the same time.

THOMPSON: Did he make it more tranquil by the way he handled it?

SCHERER: I think so.

DONOVAN: Eisenhower deliberately quieted controversy. He really loathed the New Deal and the Fair Deal. He didn't try to push reform. Nothing causes controversy like reform, and Ike was no reformer. There was no Eisenhower revolution, no great new programs that come to my mind.

DONOVAN: What did Eisenhower ever do differently from Truman or Acheson on foreign policy? He really didn't do anything differently, did he?

SCHERER: Well, he warmed up to the Russians at the very end, once Dulles was gone.

DONOVAN: Oh, yes. Détente goes back to Eisenhower.

SCHERER: He became a free agent. Then we had Mikoyan coming here, and Nixon going there, and Khrushchev coming here, and Eisenhower about to go there until the U-2 interrupted that.

DONOVAN: Let me tell you, the press knew at the time and wrote that Dulles did not want Eisenhower to go to Geneva in 1954. Eisenhower went, and that really led to the beginning of détente, without any question, I think. Then Khrushchev came here, and we had the spirit of Camp David.

KILPATRICK: It was known then that Dulles was arguing against it.

DONOVAN: Right, that was published.

KILPATRICK: The old story went that Dulles told Eisenhower that God didn't even come to earth, he sent his son, and he should stay here, too. But there was a lot written about the influence of Knowland on China policy at the time, a great deal.

SCHERER: And Styles Bridges and all that. Eisenhower could not understand Knowland; he just found him very stiff-necked and intractable.

JUERGENS: Let me ask a silly question. I think I know what the answer is going to be, and you may shoot me down. Most publications are owned by Republicans. Do you think that fact has something to do with the way presidential administrations are reported? *Time* obviously treated Eisenhower in a different way than it treated Truman. Quite aside from the fact, as you said, that the pot was always bubbling with Truman, one is tempted to feel that partisan preference had something to do with it. I'm wondering even with your paper, the *Herald Tribune*, a great newspaper but a Republican paper, whether that had something to do with your coverage?

DONOVAN: The answer, in general, is yes, although I don't think in a sinister way. The proprieters of the *Herald Tribune* were enormously interested in news about Eisenhower. But they didn't ask that it be written differently from other news. I never remember any influence from the paper on covering Eisenhower as against covering anybody else. But there was the fact that you knew you were writing to a very receptive audience in the editorial conferences. Every writer writes for editors at the beginning. Copy on Eisenhower was welcome and we'd be played well on the paper. You also knew, going back earlier into the Truman times, that the stories that made Truman look ridiculous would be great. I never wrote one that way other than what straight news coverage dictated. We had a Washington Bureau Chief, Bert Andrews, who was a star reporter in the old mold, whose day was made when he could nail Truman to the wall. The paper loved that. I don't suppose they would have loved it if Bert was nailing Eisenhower to the wall—he wasn't around then. He died in the summer of 1953.

JUERGENS: Of course what I'm leading up to is that while Eisenhower presided over a tranquil period, and was an enormously popular figure, and all the rest, is it possible that part of the reason why he had a pretty good press was—

SCHERER: The publishers liked him.

JUERGENS: The publishers liked him, and although re-porters weren't getting orders to puff him, they knew what sort of stuff their editors liked to see.

KILPATRICK: But I think the *New York Times* reporting on Eisenhower was as critical as almost any and they had supported him very vigorously. Wasn't he annoyed by the bureau's cover-age on a lot of things?

DONOVAN: Oh, yes. I'll tell you right now I can't remem-ber writing any stories on any president that were harder than those on Eisenhower over the Soviet lead on Sputnik, and I had no problems with the paper. We wrote the Sputnik story very hard on the *Herald Tribune*.

SCHERER: That was a low point in his administration. He went down to George Humphrey's place in Georgia and just sat there for about ten days.

DONOVAN: We wrote very hard on Dulles and "brinks-manship."

KILPATRICK: There was certainly a lot of hard writing about his failure to stand up to McCarthy.

DONOVAN: Oh, an awful lot of that was in the press, an awful lot, about how Ike wouldn't stand up to McCarthy—but Ike was not a very good target for reporters: he just wasn't. He rode the punches, he eschewed controversy. There was the obvious probity of the man himself: he wasn't mixed up in scandal. He had a cautious foreign policy; and I don't really remember any great changes in foreign policy.

SCHERER: You'd ask him a question with an edge in it, and he'd say, "I don't deal in personalities."

DONOVAN: Even the toughest critics who went after Ike found Ike no great target. He was a very skillful fellow in that. Let me tell you, Ike knew Washington. He'd been before con-gressional committees for years. He knew press relations from being Supreme Allied Commander. He was no easy target.

SCHERER: And he had a sweetheart relationship with Rayburn and Johnson.

DONOVAN: I don't remember any great serious attack on Eisenhower in the Congress. Ike was a kind of case by himself. Other Republican presidents have caught it from Republican papers.

JUERGENS: Historians do play the game of ranking presidents, and I think that if we were to pick one president whose reputation among historians has changed radically over the past ten or fifteen years, it would be Eisenhower. A few years back Eisenhower was talked about as the do-nothing chairman of the board. He wasn't quite bright. You thought about him in terms of reading Zane Grey novels and painting by the numbers. That, and playing bridge, were about as far as it went. But all of a sudden you have the sense that this guy was shrewd like a fox. He accomplished just what he wanted to accomplish, and if there was heat to be taken he made sure that other people took the heat. Of course, nowadays, after Vietnam, it looks very good also that we didn't get involved in wars while he was President. His stock among historians, in short, is on the rise.

DONOVAN: Everyone can have his own opinion. I didn't think Eisenhower was nearly as bad at the time as some people were saying he was, and I don't think he was as great as some people are now saying he was.

JUERGENS: You've been more consistent right along.

DONOVAN: I'm not saying if I have or not, but that's my feeling.

LATIMER: I was reminded a minute ago of something I think happened in 1956, just before the presidential campaign was getting going, when there was speculation about Richard Nixon for a second term as vice-president. My vague recollection is that it was at a press conference, and I would like to get what really happened. Did somebody ask the question and did Ike say, "Well, if you give me a week I might think of something good." Did Ike calculate that? Was it later?

SCHERER: It was later. No, that was just an inadvertance— Charlie Mohr of *Time* got up at the very end of the news conference, and the question was something like, "You have said that Dick Nixon was at the center of everything. Could you tell us one or two major things that he has done?" This was just before the 1960 election.

DONOVAN: Oh, yes. Nixon was in a rage!

SCHERER: Ike said, "Oh, I don't know, give me a week, maybe I could think of something." I don't think he so much meant to put Nixon down as—

LATIMER: Was it deliberate or not? That's what I was asking.

SCHERER: I don't think so. I don't think he had any great fondness for Nixon, but on the other hand he was not cruel enough to do that.

DONOVAN: I just think he couldn't answer the question, that was it.

SCHERER: Yes, he couldn't answer the question.

LATIMER: And he didn't realize what he was saying?

SCHERER: He didn't realize the devastating way it would come out.

KILPATRICK: It certainly hurt Nixon a great deal, there was no question about that, and I don't think Nixon ever forgot it.

LATIMER: I don't know why I thought that was in '56.

SCHERER: In '56 he had generally suggested that maybe Nixon should get off the ticket.

DONOVAN: He could carve another role for himself.

SCHERER: Maybe in the cabinet. You know, the name of Harold Stassen was surfaced, the name of Chris Herter, and there were other names floating around. Eisenhower himself told us that he could see various people as candidates for president. He mentioned Frank Lausche; he mentioned George Craig of Indiana, who later went to jail; and he mentioned one or two others. You remember that? We were astounded.

DONOVAN: Any one who could get the true story on Eisenhower's feelings on Nixon would have to be an awfully good reporter. It's very hard to do. You talk to Milton Eisenhower, and even now he will tell you one story—you talk with John Eisenhower, he will tell you the opposite. And those are two men who were very close to the late President. I think Ike respected Nixon; I think he liked him all right. Presidents never think their vice presidents are good, you know.

THOMPSON: He wouldn't have blocked him, though.

DONOVAN: Oh, no.

SCHERER: I think he resented the fact that Nixon didn't call on him. I once asked him why he didn't campaign more for Nixon in 1960 than he did, and he said, "Dick never asked me." This was in a talk we had at Gettysburg some years later. He would have liked to have been more involved in that election.

DONOVAN: He felt hurt. And as a matter of fact he advised Nixon not to go on television with Kennedy and resented for years that Nixon had turned down his advice, because that may well have cost Nixon the election. Ike was very hurt by the election of Kennedy; he was shocked and chagrined by it.

THOMPSON: We turn now to a paper by Charles Roberts on John F. Kennedy and the press.

JFK AND THE PRESS

The Beginning of a 'New Era In Political Communication'

Although it happened only a generation ago, few Americans remember or realize what a stir was created by the first presidential news conference to be televised "live" from Washington. It happened on January 25, 1961, just five days after John F. Kennedy took his oath of office.

A record crowd of 418 reporters, bathed in bright TV lights, participated in the dinner-hour show. That was 106 more than had ever before gathered for a presidential news conference.[1] An audience of 60 million watched in living rooms, dining rooms, and bar rooms across the country as the new, young President dramatically announced before 11 TV and movie cameras that the Soviet Union had released two captured U.S. airmen—a possible "break" in the cold war—and then gracefully fielded questions from 31 reporters who managed to get recognized. The show lasted 39 minutes—10 minutes longer than his aging predecessor had allowed his conferences to run—and JFK's fast-paced performance was almost flawless.

From my assigned seat, second row center in the cavernous auditorium of the then-new State Department Annex, I sensed from the moment the President walked onstage that the presidential news conference would never be the same again. It had not only become "show business"—confirming the dire predictions of recalcitrant writing reporters—it had also, as *Newsweek* noted in its next issue, opened "a new era in political communication."

News magazines, trying to give an extra-dimension to a well-covered story, are often guilty of hyperbole, but *Newsweek's* description of that conference as "momentous" and "historic"

---

[1] 312 reporters jammed the Indian Treaty Room of the old Executive Office Building on Feb. 29, 1956, to hear President Eisenhower announce whether he would run for a second term.

has stood the test of time. Kennedy's decision to go "live" changed the presidential press conference (as it was known before TV) more than any other single innovation in the 80-year history of scheduled meetings between journalists and the chief executive.

In an administration that was eventually accused of managing the news and taking reprisals against correspondents who refused to be cheerleaders, Kennedy's innovative news conference was the most successful of his many approaches to the media, so we will examine it first and then look at his other relations with the press.

The News Conference

Since some may argue that Kennedy and his press secretary, Pierre Salinger, simply adapted to the electronic age, it may be useful to look back on the conference as it existed before JFK crossed the New Frontier. President Eisenhower's press chief, Jim Hagerty, had permitted radio taping of Ike's press conferences since December 12, 1953, and filming of those conferences since January 19, 1955. In each case they were recorded for broadcast at a later hour, and Hagerty reserved the right to edit them.

In practice, Hagerty did little or no editing, but because the "canned" conferences lacked any sense of immediacy when aired several hours after the event, the networks, by 1960, were using only brief excerpts, or "highlights," of Ike's often-dull encounters with the press.

Hagerty had permitted one hastily-arranged Eisenhower press conference to be televised live. That was at the Republican National Convention in San Francisco in 1956, when Ike announced that Harold Stassen was abandoning his "dump-Nixon" drive and would second Richard Nixon's renomination for vice president.

Eager to get that harmonious word out to the delegates in a hurry, Hagerty permitted live cameras to carry the announcement and a brief question period that followed. After that the White House resumed its ban on live cameras at news conferences.

Throughout the 1950's, a decade of tense relations with Moscow, the most powerful argument against the President going on the air while actually jousting with reporters was the widely-held belief that a slip of the tongue might cause international repercussions. Kennedy's two top foreign policy advisers, McGeorge Bundy and Dean Rusk, were among those who thought that this risk outweighed the putative advantages of a live telecast.

It was just about a month before his first news conference—while he was still president-elect—that Kennedy decided to run that risk. JFK, Salinger later told me, was not only confident that he could handle foreign policy questions, but realized that *if* he slipped he could fire off a correction or clarification by the same fast medium that aired his blunder.[2]

Like many White House correspondents who had covered Eisenhower, my "beat" became President-elect Kennedy immediately after the 1960 election. (Because *Newsweek* thought Nixon would win, I was in Los Angeles, rather than Hyannis Port, that long night the votes were counted.) Salinger informed us of Kennedy's decision to go live with his press conferences at a briefing in Palm Beach, Florida, a few days after JFK had entertained us at a Christmas party in his father's oceanfront home. Despite a prevailing mood of bonhomie, print reporters—comprising the vast majority of the press corps—objected vociferously to the idea of making a "TV spectacle" out of the news conference.

Most of the correspondents summoned from poolside at the Palm Beach Towers that day had been around Washington much longer than Salinger, if not Kennedy, and thought they had a better feel of how a White House press conference should be run. Some argued that the new format would destroy the informal give-and-take of the conference—Truman had called it "rough and tumble"—while others complained it would make "actors" out of honest newsmen. This ignored the fact that many Washington correspondents had already moved in that direction with the installation of movie cameras at the Eisenhower conferences.

In Palm Beach and at a subsequent pre-inaugural working lunch with Salinger at a hotel in Washington, many of us also

---

[2] Kennedy did, in fact, bobble a foreign policy question at his first conference. He said he looked forward to a resumption of atomic "tests" when he meant atomic "talks." There were no repercussions.

objected to Pierre's proposed abolition of the rule—dating back to Truman—that a reporter should identify himself before asking a question. Salinger insisted that many correspondents sought presidential recognition at Ike's conferences just to get "free advertising" for their networks or publications. There was a germ of truth to this charge; many correspondents for provincial papers *did* feel their jobs were more secure when their names appeared with regularity in the transcripts of Ike's news conferences in the *New York Times*.

Reminding us not too tactfully that it was the *President's* conference, not ours, Salinger rejected all efforts to preserve it in *status quo*. He then went about the business of setting up the 35th President's first news conference, including arrangements for new, supersensitive "shotgun" microphones to pick up reporter's questions at long range and the assignment of 58 reserved seats for White House "regulars"—23 more than Hagerty had set aside in the old Indian Treaty Room. The rest, as they say, is history.

The live cameras transformed the "bully pulpit" of Theodore Roosevelt, the first president to meet regularly with journalists, into a podium far more powerful than anything envisioned by TR. They gave the President the upper hand forevermore in his verbal bouts with the press. And they also enabled Kennedy's successors—via satellites that were launched later—to address the chancelleries of the world, instantly and without any ambassadors as middlemen.

But, most important, the live cameras handed the President a platform from which he could speak, literally, over the heads of reporters and editors, anchormen and commentators—what JFK called the "hostile press"—directly to the voters on any issue at almost any time.

"We couldn't survive without TV," said Kennedy's special counsel, Ted Sorensen, who had also opposed the move, once he saw the implications of this breakthrough. Kennedy put it in earthier terms to a friend from the print media. "Well," he told Ben Bradlee, then my boss as Washington Bureau Chief of *Newsweek*, "I always said that when we don't have to go through you bastards, we can really get our story out to the American people."

In a euphoric mood, Kennedy clearly felt he had solved the problem posed by Bryce when he wrote at the turn of the century: "To catch and hold the attention of the people is the chief difficulty as well as the first duty of an American reformer." In fact, Kennedy liked his invention so much that he held 20 news conferences during his first year in office—in contrast with President Reagan's six during the same period.

That the American people also liked the televised sessions was documented in a survey conducted for the White House by Young & Rubicam, a New York ad agency. In June of 1962, Y&R researchers found that 95 per cent of the people they interviewed thought watching a JFK press conferences was a "worthwhile experience." Among the reasons given: The conferences were "informative" and "educational" and gave "a feeling of democracy." Surprisingly, some respondents who thought Kennedy was not doing a good job as President took a favorable view of his news conferences.

Franklin D. Roosevelt, made a similar breakthrough, from the presidential point of view, when he invented the radio "fireside chat" as a means of bypassing the press to reach the people in the depression-ridden 1930's.[3] But the televised news conference is a far more effective vehicle because, in good times or bad, a spontaneous, unrehearsed encounter with reporters will command greater attention. And although TV networks can and have refused to provide free time for presidential speeches, they are less likely to turn their backs on live news conferences, which underline their importance as purveyors of news.

Kennedy and his successors have avoided wearing out their welcome at the networks by not conducting many news conferences in prime time. Shortly after the Y&R survey, Salinger told me he had not scheduled evening conferences since JFK's debut because (1) any news the President made would miss all the morning papers and (2) it would cost the networks a lot of money in lost advertising. At that time, after 18 months in office, the audience for the President's news sessions, held mostly in the afternoon, had leveled off at about 6 million homes.

Had a president with less charisma than Kennedy first faced the press on live TV, it is possible that the televised conference would not have become a part of the presidency—a custom

---

[3] FDR used the "fireside" format sparingly, making only four such talks during his first year and only eight during his first term as President.

that all presidents are obliged to respect. But Kennedy's quick wit and facile tongue made press conference watchers out of many citizens who had never read (and never will read) transcripts of White House news conferences. Five administrations later, it is almost inconceivable that a future president, no matter how inept on camera, would risk the wrath of the media and the voters by refusing to face the press and public simultaneously on the "box."

Re-reading the transcripts of Kennedy's conferences after 20 years, one is reminded of the saying "that everyone laughs at a rich man's jokes." Some of JFK's fast rejoinders that rocked the room with laughter—even when they were designed to evade embarrassing questions—are not that funny when read today.

But it was a growing infrequency of press conferences, rather than a lack of humor in them, that brought about the first criticism of Kennedy's press relations. That was the fall of 1961 when—after weathering the Bay of Pigs fiasco and the Berlin Wall crisis—the President went from August 30 to October 11 without facing the media. Correspondents noted that this did not comport with his campaign statement of August 20, 1960, at Independence, Mo., where he said: "I would think that whoever was President would see the press at least once a week."

By November he had fallen behind Ike—who was criticized by the Democrats for eight years for the infrequency of his news conferences[4]—and I was noting in a memorandum to my editors in New York that "many reporters feel he is now less responsive to questions than President Eisenhower was. . . . The transcripts of his conferences are full of evasive filibusters."

Yet, when Bob Pierpoint, who covered the presidency for CBS for 25 years, asked a group of past and present White House correspondents to rate seven presidents—from Eisenhower through Reagan—on their press conference performances, he found that collectively we gave Kennedy the best "report card," and that JFK scored higher than the other presidents in two areas—"compative skill" and "humor."

Here is Pierpoint's survey as it appeared in the January, 17,

---

[4] With 64 news conferences in 34 months, for an average of 1.882 conferences per month, JFK finally finished behind Ike, who held 193 in 96 months for an average of 2.01 per month. Both finished far behind FDR (998 in 12 years and 3 months, 6.789 per month) and Truman (324 in 7 years and 9 months, 3.483 per month.)

1982, issue of *Parade* magazine, with each president rated in each category on a scale of 1 to 10:

	Eisenhower	Kennedy	Johnson	Nixon	Ford	Carter	Reagan
Candor	8	5	2	5	7	8	6
Informative Value	7	6	3	6	5	7	4
Combative Skill	4	9	6	8	4	6	8
Humor	3	9	4	4	6	7	8.5
Total	22	29	15	23	22	28	26.5

Was Kennedy himself satisfied with his press conferences? In one of his last meetings with reporters, after invoking poet Robert Frost, he expressed doubt that some proposed changes would improve the format that had evolved. This was the exchange:

Q.   Mr. President, have you given any thought to some of the proposals advanced from time to time for improving the presidential conference devoted all to one subject or to have written questions at a certain point?

A.   We . . . , I have heard of that, and I have seen criticism of the proposal. The difficulty is—as Mr. Frost said about not taking down a fence until you find out why it was put up—I think all the proposals made to improve it will really not improve it.

I think we do have the problem of moving very quickly from subject to subject, and therefore I am sure many of you feel that we are not going into any depth. So I would try to recognize perhaps the correspondent on an issue two or three times in a row, and we could perhaps meet that problem. Otherwise, it seems to me it serves its purpose, which is to have the President in the bulls eye, and I suppose that is in some ways revealing.

The date of the 61st conference, with its ironic reference to having the President "in the bulls eye" was September 12, 1963, just a little over two months before the President was murdered at Dallas with a rifle mounted with a telescopic gunsight.

Press Relations

Although it is the most visible part of a president's relations with the press, the news conference is by no means the end-all, be-all in that relationship. Kennedy cultivated the media in many other ways and broke new ground in some of his dealings with the journalists who chronicled the New Frontier. His overtures to the press included:

• Allowing reporters greater access to members of his White House staff than had been granted by previous administrations.

• TV "specials," including in-depth interviews with network correspondents and a tour of the White House with his wife, Jackie.

• Similar exclusives for print media, including magazine picture spreads and stories on "a day in the life of the President."

• Backgrounders at which, on a not-for-attribution basis, he revealed his thinking and described to White House "regulars" his options on major problems confronting him.

• White House luncheons for editors and publishers from the hinterlands.

• More "perks" for journalists, including invitations to lunches, state dinners, and other social functions.

Of these devices for getting a better press, the granting of access to White House staff and the TV specials were the most innovative. White House correspondents, I can testify, were most grateful for the Kennedy/Salinger decision to let reporters probe behind the walls of the lobby in the West Wing, to which we had been virtually restricted in Eisenhower's day. Where, under Ike, no reporter could see a White House staffer (Chief of Staff Sherman Adams excepted) without first "clearing" it with Jim Hagerty, under JFK it was possible to talk to key members of the Kennedy team in their offices or at lunch.

This was a break for those correspondents who wanted to go beyond the handouts distributed at Salinger's twice-daily press briefings to find out how and why presidential decisions were made. (Some newsmen who had actually slept in the lobby's overstuffed chairs during the Eisenhower Era continued to doze under Kennedy.) McGeorge Bundy (on foreign affairs), Kenneth O'Donnell (on politics), Lawrence O'Brien (on legislation), and Ted Sorensen (on JFK's mood and thinking) were invaluable sources whose names rarely appeared in the informed reporting they made possible.

The TV specials were a stunning success, from the President's point of view. At the first of them, in December of 1962, JFK got mostly friendly, or "softball" questions from three network correspondents who were apparently so grateful for their "Conversation with the President" that they entirely forgot about the adversary relationship between journalists and the chief executive. Walter Cronkite and Chet Huntley got exclusive one-on-one interviews when their CBS and NBC evening news shows switched from 15 minutes to a half-hour format, and ABC was allowed to tape a close-up of the President in his command post during his battle with Gov. George Wallace over integration of the University of Alabama.

But the real *coup,* in which the medium was used to the maximum advantage of the First Family, came when Jackie Kennedy took CBS and millions of TV viewers on an hour-long tour of the White House in 1962 to see what her "restoration" had accomplished. This show got such a build-up that ABC and NBC demanded that they be allowed to air it along with CBS. Salinger acceded to this unprecedented plea and the CBS-originated show appeared simultaneously on all three networks.

The idea of unattributable background sessions for White House "regulars" did not originate with Kennedy—Eisenhower tried them during his second term—and the two that he staged produced mixed results for JFK. Both were held on an invitation-only basis at his father's Palm Beach home during the Christmas holiday season with the idea of providing reporters with material for year-end "think pieces."

The backgrounders were divided into discussions of foreign and domestic policy. Each produced a rash of stories reflecting Kennedy's thoughts on current issues, deviously attributed to "sources close to the Administration" or "persons who have talked to the President." These circumlocutions did not fool sophisticated readers or editors, but they did produce a rash of complaints from papers that were not invited.

The luncheons for editors and publishers, invited to the White House in state and regional groups, generated some editorials that reflected a greater understanding of the President's problems. But they, too, produced some unwanted side-effects. At the lunch for Texans, E. M. (Ted) Dealey, publisher of the *Dallas Morning News*, teed off on Kennedy for being "soft" on the Soviets. He read a 500-word prepared statement calling for "a man on horseback to lead this nation," adding: "Many people in Texas and the Southwest think that you are riding Caroline's tricycle."

The White House response to this newsmaking violation of JFK's 100-proof hospitality came ten days later when Charles Bartlett, then Washington correspondent for the *Chattanooga Times*, wrote a story quoting at length from what he said was Kennedy's reply to Dealey at the luncheon. "I'm just as tough as you are, Mr. Dealey," Kennedy said, according to the Bartlett story. "And I didn't get elected by arriving at soft judgments."

Wire services that picked up the Bartlett story noted that he was a close friend of the President. He was, in fact, the man who introduced JFK to his wife, Jackie.

Dealey and several other Texas publishers denied that Kennedy made the speech Bartlett attributed to him. But, whether Dealey or Bartlett was right, the exchange illustrates another facet of JFK's relations with the press: Kennedy had more close friends among the working press in Washington than any president in memory—and he did not hesitate to use them in defense of the New Frontier.

The new President made it clear he would not turn his back on his prepresidential journalist friends when he dropped in at the home of columnist Joe Alsop in the wee hours following his inauguration and on *Newsweek*'s Ben Bradlee, a former Georgetown neighbor on his first Sunday morning as President. Among his other good friends in the press were Stewart Alsop, then Washington correspondent for the *Saturday Evening Post*, and Rowland Evans, then with the *New York Herald Tribune*.

These friendships proved mutually beneficial when JFK wanted to put out an "inside" story with the assurance that it was in friendly hands. For example, Bartlett and Stewart Alsop wrote for the *Saturday Evening Post* an all-but-authorized behind-the-scenes account of how the Cuban missile crisis was handled. Bradlee and I, with access to FBI files, collaborated on a *Newsweek* piece that put down what we called the "John's other wife" story—a widely-circulated rumor that JFK had been secretly married to the thrice-married Newport socialite before he met Jacqueline Bouvier. The *Newsweek* story was far more effective than a White House denial would have been.

But the Kennedy's close friends in the press were not the only journalists to benefit by his presidency. Because of greater access to him and his advisers, all of us were able to write more authoritatively during the early days of his administration. And during the Thousand Days of Camelot, reporters were romanced with invitations to glittering state dinners, luncheons, and receptions at the White House on a scale unmatched by previous administrations.

Unlike the Eisenhower days—when Ike talked to us like supply troops, a sort of necessary appendage to his command—there was almost a spirit of camaraderie among White House staff and press, particularly during the first-year "honeymoon." This is a dangerous position for journalists to get in; it can numb their critical faculties. However, JFK was our age, knew a lot about our business[5], and seemed genuinely interested in our work and our families.None of us regarded his friendliness as phony or his hospitality as a mere gambit to get a better press. The first strains in this relationship occurred a few months into the new administration when it became apparent to some of us that Kennedy was not only the friendliest, but the most thin-skinned of presidents. Although JFK and his aides were quick to compliment a reporter on a "good story," i.e., one favorable to the administration, they were intolerant of any criticism. What was worse, reporters who wrote stories that annoyed the White House suddenly found that their sources of information were drying up. Those staffers who had been so accessible were suddenly too busy to talk. Phone calls went unreturned.

"You are either for us or against us," is the way Kenny O'Donnell, the President's appointments secretary, put it to me.

What the White House wanted in the press room, obviously, were cheerleaders, not skeptical reporters. The carrot and stick treatment extended even to such presidential friends as *Newsweek*'s Bradlee, who, for example, was chewed out first by the President and then his brother, the Attorney General, for a story that the administration was preparing to put a Massachusetts political hack (who had worked for the Kennedys) on the

---

[5] He was a reporter briefly for Hearst's International News Service following World War II and a voracious reader of newspapers and periodicals.

federal bench. The story was true; what the Kennedys resented was that it was embarrassing.

The UPI's Merriman Smith, then the "dean" of White House correspondents, marvelled at how the White House could spot an unfavorable paragraph in a paper of 3,000 circulation 2,000 miles away. "They must have a thousand little gnomes reading the papers for them," said Smitty.

The public first became aware of JFK's hypersensitivity, I think, when the story leaked out in the spring of 1962 that the President had cancelled the White House's daily order for 22 copies of the *New York Herald Tribune*, a staunchly Republican paper that had carried several less-than-flattering stories about the Kennedys. One was a story about their lavish entertainment at Mt. Vernon for the president of Pakistan. The emphasis of the story was on the cost rather than what a grand party it was. Another was the *Trib*'s handling of the Billie Sol Estes case, a grain storage scandal in Texas.

It was in the wake of this petulant move that Kennedy was asked at his May 9 press conference about his attitude toward the press and replied that he was "reading more and enjoying it less." He added, with apparent resignation, that reporters were "doing their task, as a critical branch, the Fourth Estate and I am attempting to do mine, and we are going to live together for a period of time and then go our separate ways."

The story of the White House press corps' disenchantment with Kennedy broke into the open three months later when *Look* magazine, in a spread entitled "Kennedy vs. the Press," reported that 25 or 30 Washington correspondents had been reprimanded by members of the Kennedy family or White House staff or been questioned by the FBI or Pentagon security officers. Several complained that the White House had put "the freeze" on them for stories that did not pass the test of friendliness.

In fairness, *Look* reported that of about 100 correspondents it questioned, about half took a "lighthearted view of the Kennedy administration's knuckle rapping of the press." The rest saw it as a serious attempt to pressure them. Still, *Look*, which had its share of favors from the Kennedy White House, concluded that the press had taken "almost as many lumps in 19 months of Kennedy rule as in the previous three administrations put together."

The situation got worse that fall when for several weeks in the aftermath of the Cuban missile crisis officials at all levels of the

White House, State Department, and Pentagon became totally uncommunicative. To make sure they remained uncommunicative, the Pentagon and State Department ordered their officials to report in writing on any contact they had with reporters.

No reporter I know faulted Kennedy for managing the news while he and Soviet Premier Khrushchev were "eyeball to eyeball" at the brink of a nuclear war over the question of Russian missiles in Cuba. But when the embargo on *all* information concerning negotiations with Moscow and the U.S. blockade of Cuba continued long after Khruschev had agreed to remove his missiles, the press perceived, as the *New York Times* put it, that it was "being used more often than informed."

This feeling was reinforced when the Pentagon's chief spokesman, Arthur Sylvester, told an interviewer that "the generation of news by the government becomes a weapon in a strained situation," and then added in a subsequent speech that the government had a right "if necessary, to lie to save itself when it is going up in a nuclear war." Both of Sylvester's statements were arguably true, but they did not improve Kennedy's relations with the press.

Arthur Krock, the venerable Washington oracle of the *New York Times* and a onetime mentor of JFK, wrote: "A news management policy not only exists, but in the form of direct and deliberate action, has been enforced more cynically and boldly than by any previous administration in a period when the U.S. was not at war."[6] At his next press conference following the missile crisis—his first in ten weeks—Kennedy seemed to concede that his administration had gone too far down the road of news management. He defended, of course, the close-mouthed handling of troop movements and intelligence data, but promised to "see if we can get this straightened out so that there is a free flow of news to which the press is entitled and which I think ought to be in the press, and on which any administration really must depend as a check to its own actions."

Apparently, the press's critical reporting of the Washington news blackout had served as a check on the President.

---

[6] *Fortune* magazine, March, 1963.

Requiem

The bullet that killed President Kennedy made him a hero, posthumously, to all but the most dyed-in-the-wool Kennedy haters. His martyrdom assured him, at least temporarily, a better niche in history than he might have earned by serving out his first, and perhaps a second, term.

Now historians and biographers are taking a harder look at his brief tenure. They are finding, in many cases, that his rhetoric was better than his record. They are also finding character defects. His celebrated war record and his sole authorship of two books are questioned. It is revealed that he lied about the state of his health and that he taped phone conversations with unwitting White House callers, including newsmen. Worst of all, there is persuasive evidence that he was a compulsive—and indiscriminate—philanderer.

These disclosures raise some troubling questions for journalists. If Kennedy's shortcomings were known or suspected—as many were—why weren't they reported more effectively? Was Arthur Krock right when he charged that JFK managed the news by "selective personal patronage" and "social flattery" of Washington correspondents and commentators? Were we the victims, rather than the beneficiaries, of briefings and contacts with JFK that left us in a "state of protracted enchantment evoked by the President's charm and the aura of his office?"

Most reporters who covered Kennedy would, I think, acknowledge that these questions are valid, but argue that to pose them now—particularly the problem of Kennedy's peccadillos—is to ask them out of context. In the pre-Watergate days of Camelot, most reporters on the White House beat, I believe, though that what a president did in his spare time was his own business—if he wanted it that way, and provided his extra-curricular activities did not impair his effectiveness as chief executive. Some also lived by the Biblical injunction: Let him who is without sin cast the first stone.

As for Krock's charge, there is no denying that Kennedy flattered and charmed the press by his attentions. What is debatable is the extent to which we were rendered uncritical. The fact that reams were written about JFK's attempts to manage the news is certainly evidence in mitigation of the charge. If we were captivated, we at least protested profusely while the seduction was in progress. But most of us now reaffirm what we knew then: that an arms-length relationship (such as we had under Ike) is better for both the journalist and his readers. Whether it should also be an *adversary* relationship is a topic for another day.

The irony of what is happening now is that as estimates of Kennedy's presidency go down, his marks for skillful handling of the press must be revised upward. If his presidency is to be branded as mediocre—if his administration got a much better press than it deserved—then he must be acknowledged as the greatest manupulator of the media since FDR and an even greater communicator than Ronald Reagan. One thing is certain: Whatever his motive, his distinction as the first president to admit the public via television to the White House press conference is secure. He did open "a new era in political communication."

LYNDON B. JOHNSON AND RICHARD M. NIXON

THOMPSON: I propose now we consider two more recent presidents, Johnson and Nixon.

KILPATRICK: I might start by reading a paragraph from Jonathon Daniels, who died the other day, as you know, and who was Roosevelt's last press secretary and then for a few weeks Truman's. He said in a speech once,

> My belief is that every newspaperman should recognize himself and his duty as that of a peeping Tom. It's his business to peep and look and find and turn up the carpet to see the dirt that's been swept under there. When he ceases to do that, when he writes only pundit pieces about Afghanistan, then he's not a newspaperman, he's just playing with himself. If the press isn't there to peek, then vigilance is lost in America.

And I would like to read one more paragraph and this from Bill Greider's article in the *Atlantic* on David Stockman. Greider says that in granting him the interview, Stockman, who is a student of history,

> ... believed that he was contributing to history's record, and perhaps influencing its conclusions. For him our meetings were another channel among many he used to the press. The older generation of orthodox Republicans distrusted the press. Stockman was one of the younger new conservatives who cultivated contacts with columnists and reporters, who saw the news media as another useful tool in political combat.

I think those two paragraphs help us understand the press failures of the Johnson and Nixon administrations. Every president, as we've heard all morning, resents the criticisms of the press. But some, at least, understand that criticism is a function of the press, and that it can be useful as well as destructive. Neither Johnson nor Nixon fully understood the press; or rather, I guess I should say that Johnson understood it least of all. Nixon understood it better but he did not use it properly.

Johnson was one of the sharpest men intellectually to be

President in recent years; he was never a fool. He understood the Senate like no other. He knew how the bureaucracy operated in a very detailed and expert way. He knew where the lobbyists were and how to make use of them. But he did not understand the press. I think it was because his political career was developed in the climate of the Texas press, and it was really a docile press on the whole, in those days—not now I think. If LBJ could establish good relations with a publisher, he could be sure that reporters on that paper would treat him kindly. Only a few could not be brought into line. Yet Johnson always thought that by inviting the critics to a party or giving them a scoop he could extract teeth. When he entered the White House his foolish thought was that if he buttered up the White House correspondents the way he had buttered up the Texas press, all would be cozy. It was not to be. Reporters went about their business of scrutinizing Johnson's proposals, his appointments, and his associates.

In those early days, the *Washington Post*, which I was working for, was extremely friendly to Johnson, supported him on his Great Society proposals and on Vietnam. He should have been extremely happy to have a paper with that influence in the nation's capital, but on more than one occasion, he lectured me on how unfair the paper was, how Kay Graham and I were out to get him. He put nearly everything on a personal basis, and many of the complaints he had were about things that neither Kay nor I had any knowledge of or anything to do with. They were unimportant items on the whole. One day our State Department reporter wrote a story that was about two paragraphs long, and was buried way inside the paper. It reported that Johnson would name U. Alexis Johnson Ambassador to Japan. I had not seen the story when Johnson grabbed me in front of a good many of my colleagues and lit into me in the most violent way. I really didn't know at first what he was talking about.

On another occasion *Newsweek* reported in a Periscope item that he would name Ellsworth Bunker Ambassador to Vietnam. I suppose he could not find the *Newsweek* correspondent, and he called me into his office and read me the riot act, and denied that he had any such intention. Of course he named Bunker a few weeks later. He went on at great length about how the *Post* was out to destroy him. I repeatedly tried to say that we supported him 90 per cent of the time; he never heard me. When the *Post* shifted its position on Vietnam and became more critical on other issues, he denounced it with a cold fury, refusing to see Kay Graham altogether.

I looked up the other day some notes I made on a meeting I had with him on June 30, 1965. It was a long session, but the reason he called me in (I always thought) was to talk about George Reedy, who had succeeded Salinger as press secretary. Reedy was one of the finest men ever to serve any politician, and he was also a man of strong and brilliant intellect. He had worked for a number of years for Johnson when he was senator and vice president. But he was really not an effective press secretary, partly because he was a rather shy and withdrawn person and partly because he had been browbeaten by Johnson for too long. And now I will quote from a memo I wrote after that meeting:

> Johnson said he had had a terrible blow today. He had gotten a five page handwritten letter from George Reedy saying he would have to resign. Johnson said that Dr. James Cain of Mayo's had had Reedy at Walter Reed hospital and told him he would have to have his legs operated on and might lose one or both of them. Reedy suffered from 'hammertoes'—I don't know exactly what it is, but his toes turned in. His father had suffered from them, and I understand one of George's sons does, too. We knew that George was in pain, and Johnson said he'd been in terrible pain. Then the President said, 'I'm going to put Bill Moyers in for a week as press secretary and then try Busby in it for a while and see which one works out. Later I might bring in somebody from outside.' He said that Moyers now didn't have anything to do. I laughed—I didn't realize that he was not kidding. I thought he was kidding about Moyers, who was working eighteen hours a day. But Johnson was very upset when I laughed, and he said that everybody complained that he overworked people, that he never did that, he never overworked anybody.

Well, as you know, he named Moyers, and he did not name Busby or go through this plan to change, although he later brought in Bob Fleming for a few months, and finally George Christian. And I think that Christian was, from the point of view of Johnson, and maybe from the point of view of the press, the best press secretary that Johnson had. I asked a friend of mine the other day who had worked in the administration about this, and he said, "Johnson knew that Bill Moyers was very ambitious, and that's why he didn't want to keep him around. And he knew that George Christian's only ambition was to get back to Texas."

SCHERER: Can I interject? You said he wanted to talk to you about Reedy; what point was he trying to make?

KILPATRICK: He said, "George wants to go and teach. I told him he couldn't make a living teaching. You know, George doesn't have but eight dollars." That was the way he talked. And he said, "I want him to stay in the White House and do some work for me, but he says he will be embarrassed. And the press will ridicule him." And I said, "No sir, that's not true; the press won't ridicule him, and he won't be embarrassed." I said, "They all like him and respect him." And I think that he was looking for somebody to say that. Then he did keep George in there for quite a while, as a special assistant. I think I was a sounding board, though why he called me, I haven't any idea. He called me in and made that comment and never said it was off the record. I told my editors about it. I said, "Well, I don't think we're at liberty to write anything about it," and we didn't. I'm sure that in today's climate we would have gone with that story immediately, but we waited for him to make the announcement. Maybe that's poor newspaper work. Obviously Johnson was not going to subscribe to either Jonathan Daniels' press philosophy or to David Stockman's.

Certainly Nixon was not either, although he understood the press, I think, a little better. Nixon had fought the press almost from the beginning, and the fight started not because the press was anti-Nixon, but because Nixon was a very controversial figure when he ran for Congress and then for senator in California. He made very extravagant charges against his opponents and the press took those up and criticized him. Nixon resented all this very deeply, and while he tried at times to be conciliatory, he was never able to relax with the press, or any other group for that matter, or to work effectively with the press.

Ron Ziegler was Nixon's only press secretary whereas Johnson had about five in all, counting Salinger, and Bob Fleming for a short time. And in many ways Ziegler represented Nixon quite well. Tumulty, it seems to me, was one of the few press secretaries who really didn't sound like the president—Hagerty certainly reflected Eisenhower's thoughts; Salinger, Kennedy's; Ziegler, Nixon's; Christian reflected Johnson's thinking very accurately. Tumulty was certainly not of the Wilson mould. He was the one exception to my rule that they all sound like the man they are speaking for. Ziegler tried very hard, and certainly he's been criticized more than any other press secretary. And yet he was under severe limitations from Nixon and Haldeman. He was a good organizer in the same sense that Hagerty was. His staff hated him because he could be a martinet, but he did know how to organize trips, campaigns and so on. He understood in a limited extent Stockman's philosophy, and he put together great bundles of materials to explain certain Nixon policies—pre-Watergate.

I remember once we went to Oklahoma at the height of the Watergate crisis and Nixon spoke in a big football stadium about eight o'clock Saturday night. We, all who were traveling with him, were sure we'd get a good story, that he'd say something that would be important. And writing on a Saturday night for a Sunday morning paper is a great strain because you have very little time since you have earlier deadlines. And Nixon went to a tremendous reception. You were talking about crowds this morning. Nixon always got big crowds, tremendous crowds. There must have been 50 thousand people there all around that stadium. He made just a typical Nixon speech, just mouthing the same things he had said in other speeches and never getting on any substantive subject. All of the reporters after the speech were trying desperately to find something to write a story about, and I had finally finished a very poor one. Zeigler came up and said, "What did you think of it?" I said, "For heaven's sakes, Ron, here it is Saturday night. You've got every Sunday paper in the country and he gets up there and he doesn't have even one paragraph in his speech that's new that we can write a story about." And he hit me on the shoulder and he said, "We don't care what you write. Every television station in the country tomorrow is going to have pictures of this huge reception." Well, that wasn't enough to save Nixon, obviously, but that was the way Zeigler was thinking then in terms of the impact of television and the huge crowds cheering Nixon, even though the rest of the country was very critical of him.

Both Johnson and Nixon certainly looked on the press conference as an ordeal. I don't think any two people ever worried more about how they would do in a press conference. Of course Johnson came in after Kennedy, and Kennedy had been effective in the press conference. Johnson had strange, strange

quirks. He wouldn't go to that auditorium in the State Department because the stage was about twenty feet from the audience and he said he couldn't talk that far to people. He wanted
them right up around him; if he could get them right up against
him he could talk.

SCHERER: Plus the fact that Kennedy had used it.

KILPATRICK: And Kennedy had used the State Department
auditorium. Johnson tried to work out various ways of holding
press conferences. He held them without any notice at all. You
never knew when you went to lunch whether you would miss a
press conference.

DONOVAN: In fact, he might do his best to have one then.

KILPATRICK: He might. One day there was some bill affecting
the District of Columbia that he was to sign. The City Desk on
our paper was very eager to know exactly when he would sign,
not because they wanted a scoop (because it was something
that Johnson had advocated and we knew he would sign it), but
we just wanted to know when it would be. I asked George
Christian and he said, "Well, I'll ask the President." He came
back and he said, "He says he won't do it until Congress comes
back." They were on a four-day recess or something. So I
assured the City Desk they could relax, and the next morning
he signed the bill. There must have been a dozen, a score of
instances where I would mislead my editors on little things that
were not important, and yet I would be the one that looked like
a damn fool who didn't know what he was talking about. I think
Johnson took a certain pleasure in this.

The most famous of those instances was just after he became
President. He was in Texas over the Christmas holidays and he
was working on the budget. He had us in at least for four or five
sessions to tell us that you can't keep this budget under a
hundred billion dollars, there's just no way—it's going to be a
hundred and four or a hundred and three. We all wrote that and
sure enough, he came with a budget of 98 billion. And that's
how the credibility gap began.

DONOVAN: Are you the one who coined the term Credibility Gap?

KILPATRICK: No, Murrey Marder is the one on our paper
who first used it, but that was in reference to foreign policy.
Johnson resented it because the newspapers wrote that he was
not at ease in foreign policy, and he kept saying how many

foreign leaders he had met, how many countries he had visited, and so on. Nixon, on the other hand, was much more at ease on foreign policy issues than on domestic, and he was really not interested in many domestic issues.

Johnson was gregarious, he was fun to be with if he was in a good mood. He would talk you to death; sometimes it would be hours when you couldn't get away from him. Nixon was exactly the opposite. I have never known a politician who was as "ungregarious" as Nixon; he just disliked meeting people. There's a story that shortly after he became President, Bill Rogers, his Secretary of State, brought Elliot Richardson over for a conference. Nixon took an instant dislike to him and said, "Never bring that man back again." Rogers said, "I have to; he's Undersecretary of State and you've got to recognize that he's a man of some substance." So he finally accepted him. Well, all these qualities you're familiar with, and they were reflected in the way their press secretaries and their press operations were in those days.

THOMPSON: What about regularity of press conferences?

KILPATRICK: Neither was terribly regular. Johnson was a little more regular than Nixon—not a lot, I guess.

JUERGENS: Did you get any extra heat because you were White House correspondent for the *Post* at the time that Woodward and Bernstein were bringing a certain amount of unhappiness to the White House?

KILPATRICK: Well, that was during Nixon's time. I surely did. Often in the late afternoon they would give me their stories and say, "Go to the White House and get a reaction." Usually it was five o'clock and Zeigler would jump all over me, asking, "Why bring it in at this hour when you know I can't get an answer in time?" So I was taking the heat from both sides on that.

JUERGENS: Were there ever any ways, petty or otherwise, that you felt they tried to punish the *Post* through you?

KILPATRICK: Oh, they did, yes.

BLACKFORD: Since the last time I talked to you about it, have you found out who tried to tell the *Post* that Linwood Holton was going to be the vice president?

KILPATRICK: No, I know who told them; I'm just not at liberty to say. It was a very prominent Republican that told us that Linwood Holton was going to be nominated vice president by Nixon that afternoon.

BLACKFORD: To replace Agnew.

KILPATRICK: This was a very prominent man.

JUERGENS: May I follow up that question with a related one? I'm curious to get a *Washington Post* man's reaction as to why your paper was out in front on the Watergate story, and, when you think about it, stayed alone for quite awhile. Why do you think other newspapers and the network news took so long to pick up on the story? I can't remember the chronology, but it seems to me that it must have been several weeks.

KILPATRICK: That's a correct interpretation. I'm not sure that I know. It was a very difficult story to begin with, to get information on. We had two very aggressive reporters who were backed by the newspaper, by the editor, who spent a lot of time with them, and sub-editors who did, too, and they encouraged them to go. And I think the other papers simply weren't as aggressive as the *Post* was. Maybe Bob has something else.

DONOVAN: No, I don't.

KILPATRICK: The *Times* assigned a man to the story, exclusively, I've forgotten when, maybe late August or September. He never caught up. Some of the networks like CBS didn't.

SCHERER: Cronkite did a long piece about it during the election period.

KILPATRICK: Yes, but the day-by-day details of it—

DONOVAN: Partly it was a local police story.

KILPATRICK: It was a local police story.

DONOVAN: The other papers from out of town didn't cover police headquarters.

KILPATRICK: That's right, every time you got hold of another name, Segretti, for example, you'd start talking to him and talking to his friends, and you'd come up with another name. It took a lot of manpower to do this, and a lot of piecing together of seemingly irrelevant pieces of information.

SCHERER: The quick answer is that the *Post* had such a head start that it was difficult to catch up with their momentum and it was a hard story for TV to do.

KILPATRICK: Very hard story for TV, because nobody was going to appear on camera and talk. And it was, as Bob said, a local police story.

JUERGENS: Only at the very beginning.

KILPATRICK: The *Post* had good sources in the FBI and in

other police organizations there and I think they got a lot of information that way. And those two reporters deserve all the credit they got for just being persistent. I didn't believe a lot they were writing at first, and I was surprised by it.

JUERGENS: I was curious whether part of the reason might have been something so petty as concern by other papers and the networks that if they picked up the chase with the *Post*, they would in a way be giving publicity to a rival. They would be making the story seem more important.

SCHERER: It doesn't work that way.

KILPATRICK: I don't think so. They were all eager to get in on it; and either they didn't assign enough manpower to it or they didn't have some of the access that we did.

THOMPSON: Did either Johnson or Nixon hold stag dinners or other dinners for reporters of the kind you talked about?

KILPATRICK: Nixon never did—he did when he was vice president.

THOMPSON: Is there any way that through the Vietnam war as it began to build up more and more, it would have been possible for somebody like Johnson to keep the spotlight on the more positive things that he did?

KILPATRICK: Not on a thing as wrenching as that war was. I don't think there's anything in a public relations sense that he could have done. He had the press with him. I was thinking about it the other day. He made this speech at Hopkins in '65. We'd gotten fairly well into the war, and he made a conciliatory speech that he wanted to meet with Ho Chi Minh and give economic aid and so on. Johnson always said, "I can work with Harry Byrd and I can work with Bill Knowland and I can work with Mollie Malone in the Senate and we can always work out a compromise." He thought he could do the same thing here. I think that was the fatal philosophical point of view that he took, and he could never, never get any negotiation with Ho Chi Minh that was meaningful on the terms we put forward.

SCHERER: That's true of his whole career; he tried to manipulate everything the way he could manipulate the Senate. He was made to order for the Senate.

KILPATRICK: He was absolutely brilliant in the Senate, there's no question about it.

SCHERER: Because of the institution?

KILPATRICK: I asked Hubert Humphrey once how LBJ was

so successful and he almost laughed at me. He said, "Don't you know? He's a walking FBI. He knows the strength and weakness of every member of this body and he plays on it."

FORD, CARTER AND REAGAN

THOMPSON: Let's move on to the three most recent presidents: Ford, Carter and Reagan.

SCHERER: Well, I'll skip through Ford, who had pretty good press relations because he was a nice guy; and Carter, who held press conferences regularly and was good at it, although a bit dull, but finally just gave it up, stopped doing it. Remember that session we had with his press secretary? We asked Jody why he stopped, and Jody said, "We just thought they weren't helping us."

If I can now bring it to Reagan, one might say that Reagan has a growing reputation as a great communicator, but you won't get much agreement on that out of the White House press corps. They don't find him to be a great communicator. He's held only five formal news conferences in the first ten months; this is less than any other chief executive in the last fifty years. As I think Bob mentioned, at this point Truman had held fifty news conferences in his presidency. Reporters, by and large, admire Reagan's courtesy and his good humor, but they find that providing access to the press is not very high among Reagan's priorities. So they've become frustrated and they seize upon every occasion when he's within earshot to throw questions. They badger him at photo opportunities and Reagan has a lot of these. When pictures are taken, Sam Donaldson or Helen Thomas or somebody will shout something and Reagan will say "Hey?" and more often than not give them an answer.

The other problem of the White House correspondents, as I understand it from talking to them, is compounded by the fact that the White House has two spokesmen: Larry Speakes and Dave Gergen. They alternate and they sometimes contradict each other. I think that Reagan himself does fairly well in news conferences when he takes the time to be thoroughly briefed, but he stubbed his toe badly on the third one in which he was rather wobbly on foreign policy questions, and then there was a long hiatus before we had another one.

As you all know, we made recommendations to the "next president" (who turned out to be Reagan) last year, and we were given a lot of credit at the beginning, perhaps inordinate credit, because of a certain amount of mystery about our report, at having turned in a report and how Reagan's staff was following it.[1] The main theme which we laid out in our report is that he should hold press conferences frequently—at least once a month, maybe twice a month on television, but in some form every week. One of the more minor points we made was that he could bring some decorum into the news conference by having people hold up their hand, which of course they adopted. We also said another way to do it was to hold a lottery, which they tried. So I would have to say that although we received a lot of credit for having made good recommendations, he hasn't followed the main one.

This has all been summed up in a very, very concise and sapient way by our old friend David Broder. If you don't mind, some of you may have missed it, so I will quickly read it. I think he's caught Reagan's press conference in one piece here, very distinctly. This was written November 15 for the *Washington Post*, after the fifth news conference. Quoting now:

> President Reagan asked reporters at his news conference last week to remember that the words they write are read all around the world and to consider whether the message they send is helpful or destructive to the nation's interest.
>
> Whatever you think of that plea, the fact is that one of the most important messages is the one the President himself conveyed by his words and demeanor on public occasions. For the most part those appearances have been helpful to Reagan in advancing his goals. His wit, his good nature, and his rehearsed eloquence stand him in good stead, whether he is delivering a toast at a banquet, a brief political speech, or a televised policy address.
>
> But at the last two news conferences, the impression has been created of a man under great strain. The comments on Capitol Hill and at Embassies suggest that the tension and anxiety the President displays, when answering questions about his policies, are beginning to cause concern among those here and abroad who look to the White House for leadership.
>
> The same anxiety is being expressed by members of the White House staff, who have come to view each press conference as a hurdle that

---

[1]Editor's note: This report is reprinted in its entirety as Appendix A.

must be negotiated with care. They have adopted what my colleague Martin Schram accurately described as a damage control philosophy, for dealing with the press conferences: scheduling them infrequently, slowing down the pace of questioning by lengthy answers, and hoping that Reagan gets out of them without hurting himself.

That is a defensible if obviously defensive strategy. The practical problem is that the President is so strained in executing it, hesitant in manner and nervous in speech, that he undercuts the effort to build confidence in his leadership. The relaxed sense of command and self-control that he communicated so advantageously in his 1980 campaign debates and in almost every formal speech he has made as President, turns into a very tentative and tense performance in the press conferences.

Explanations abound. Some say the President's hearing impairment forces him to strain to hear the questions and puts him on edge even before he gives his answers. His aides have tried to reduce this problem by installing an amplifier in his podium.

Others say it is the mental gymnastics of the news conference that the President finds intimidating. He works best when he knows the topic in advance and has his index cards at hand with the points he wants to make. In the news conferences he held in his eight years as governor of California the custom was to exhaust one topic before shifting to a new one. He seemed more comfortable with that more structured format.

His critics put forward a much harsher theory: Reagan is under strain because he has such a shaky grasp of the policies for which he is formally responsible that he has a dickens of a time remembering what he was supposed to say about such and such a subject.

If that is right then we are really in for trouble, not just this administration but this country and the world. Before accepting that gloomy conclusion, I would like to see how Reagan would do if he were holding a press conference of some kind every week.

Here he gets back to what we recommended a year ago.

He did when he was governor but as President he has held only five conferences in ten months. On that schedule every one becomes a very big deal, a big mental hurdle.

The Reagan we have seen at the last couple of news conferences reminds me of the uptight, unhappy Reagan of the Iowa Caucus period 1980 when his then manager John Sears was trying to shield him from the press and public. When Reagan campaigned infrequently and under serious constraints, he was a lousy campaigner, always on the defensive. When he was unleashed in New Hampshire he was terrific.

So it is, as I suspect, with the news conference. People like my colleague Lou Cannon who covered him in California remember those gubernatorial news conferences not as ordeals to which Reagan submitted but as opportunities that he exploited easily to carry his message to the people.

The final paragraph, and this is the core of what Broder is suggesting, is again very parallel to what we said a year ago.

> Maybe he's lost the knack, now that he's ten years older, but my guess is that he's just not getting enough practice to feel comfortable in the news conference format. If he had a regular schedule where on alternating weeks he would have big televised news conferences, and small Oval Office interviews with some of the White House regulars, my guess is that he would be better briefed by his staff on a wide variety of issues, and much better prepared to discuss them. . . .

KILPATRICK: Very good—a very good column, I thought.
SCHERER: A very good column. I think he's got the heart of it—
DONOVAN: What reaction is there going to be? I wonder what White House reactions are going to be on it?
SCHERER: I don't know, I haven't heard any. . . . I think he is uncomfortable with foreign policy, and until he gets comfortable and can be easy with that he will want to shy away from them. The question is, can he or will he take time to be briefed?
BLACKFORD: Is there evidence whether *he* feels uncomfortable, or the troika feels that he may fall on his face if he has too many of them?
SCHERER: I didn't think he looked quite as uncomfortable as Dave writes, though I agree with most of it. I think the average guy looking at his news conferences and seeing him at ease, thinks he's probably come out ahead. I think it's professionals, the foreign policy experts, who tend to fault him.
ROGAN: Well, should presidential ability really be judged by the way a president deals with press conferences? Seemingly we are sitting here saying that Johnson didn't do a very good job, and other presidents were not comfortable. We wonder whether Reagan can speak on the subjects. How does the public get a measure of the man?
KILPATRICK: I think Ray is right, it's the foreign policy experts. I thought it was a very poor press conference, but I think that the average American thought he was terrific. He was very good humored. He stumbles over words, which makes you think that he is not sure of a subject, and I don't think the average voter in Podunk is going to fault him on that. They like his approach, they think he is trying to balance the budget and cut taxes and here these people are asking him these nasty questions.

DONOVAN: An awful lot of people see those conferences, and I imagine that that is reflected somewhat in the Gallup poll. People in part form their impressions of the President this way.

LATIMER: It's not original with me, but I just have the theory, and I don't know who originated it, that the format of the press conference is made to order for the President on television: He is there fighting off the wolves and defending the country.

BLACKFORD: That's what's so ironic.

LATIMER: You don't have to be too skillful when there is no coordination out there among all the questioners to look pretty good in that press conference.

KILPATRICK: And the public doesn't sympathize with the reporter who asks some nasty question; they sympathize with the president more often than not.

BLACKFORD: Is there such a thing today as the "regulars" as there was in the Eisenhower administration?

SCHERER: It's bigger, much bigger.

BLACKFORD: You talk 15 people—my God, how many are there now?

SCHERER: Well, the intimacy is gone, but you can recapture some of that, I think. The networks do want access, but if the president says, "I'm going to do it, just standing around the desk," they'd have to go along, and they would. They'd rather have that access than none.

LATIMER: Of course, Reagan was unfortunately out of action for six or eight months there. Would it have been different if he had not been shot and severely wounded? Would the press conferences have been held more often? Would he be communicating any more? Would we be any better off?

SCHERER: I think somewhat more, but his tendency is to do it as often as you have to to get away with it, so to speak.

YOUNG: Is this because you think he's gotten a bad press on his press conferences? It changes his pattern that he had in California. Negative assessments, by not only the reporters dealing with foreign policy, but domestic policy as well, have apparently gotten more negative the more he had. So, might it not be, even though the public might think he's doing fine, that the fact that it produces bad assessments might be self-perpetuating?

SCHERER: Well, I think they crank those in. Back to our lunch with Jody Powell, we said to him that it's one of the things we felt Carter did fairly well. He was always in command of his facts, he rarely made a booboo, and he came well briefed. We asked, "Why didn't you do it more often?" Powell said, "We just didn't think they were good for us." And it's conceivable that Baker, Meese, and Deaver have made this judgment.

THOMPSON: Helen Thomas asked the theatrics question the other day—Was the budget theatrics?—and President Reagan bridled a little.

SCHERER: I think what it amounts to is he can get by with it with the people on manner. He is so winning, likeable that he can get away with being inarticulate or even off base on foreign policy, but he gets faulted by the experts, the people who write in Washington.

JUERGENS: If I may say something pretty obvious, Broder's column makes me wonder what would I recommend to President Reagan if I were one of his aides. Broder points out there are a couple of possibilities. One is that the President is just getting out of practice. The other, of course, is that he is not very well informed, and press conferences pose all sorts of perils for him. If I were President Reagan's assistant and I had reason to believe that the problem was the second possibility, namely that he doesn't know what's going on, then I suppose my recommendation would be to forget what all of these goodhearted commissions are saying to you and stay away from press conferences. You have nothing to gain from them and you have a lot to lose. So, see Barbara Walters periodically, and don't have any weaknesses highlighted.

KILPATRICK: That's why I asked you that question this morning, I was thinking about that.

JUERGENS: Yes, and I was thinking about it too. You see, there's something implicit in everything I've been saying. The press conference can be a useful tool for a president who truly knows what's going on. President Wilson, whatever else you might say about him, was informed. Franklin Roosevelt was informed. You spoke this morning about Harry Truman— on most issues he was informed. I'm not sure about President Reagan. One gets the impression that perhaps he is not working as hard as he might; perhaps he's not keeping on top of things. . . .

SCHERER: He has no depth, as it were.

JUERGENS: I was struck, for example, by this hassle we had where Haig said one thing about contingency plans and Weinberger another. Now, the very next day President Reagan had a conference, and you didn't need a lot of professional acumen to know that there was going to be a question on that. And Reagan hadn't prepared anything. He responded, "Well, I'll have to look into that. . . . "

SCHERER: It must have been prepared: I think he forgot it or something.

DONOVAN: Just for the record here, I'm convinced that some of these pre-press conference briefings of the President have had a lot to do, suddenly, with firming up things in the White House. An occasion comes to mind that has never been publicized yet, but during the Truman scandals, there was an episode in which Attorney General Howard McGrath fired Newbold Morris, a New York attorney who had been brought into the administration to clean up the scandals. At first Truman was inclined to temporize with the firing of Morris. But at the pre-press conference briefing, his press people said, "Look, you've got to do something about this thing because you're going to be put on the spot here in one hour." Truman still tried to ride the situation out for a while, but all of a sudden picked up the telephone and fired Howard McGrath and was then prepared at the press conference to say that McGrath had resigned. I'm sure a lot of things have been firmed up in those conferences when aides say to a president, "You're going to be asked about this: Now what *is* our policy?"

YOUNG: Bill Safire's column made basically the same point. He said the infrequency of press conferences means that a president is not subjecting himself to that housekeeping and that identification of decision options, the action-forcing processes that go along with the pre-briefing for the press conferences. As I understood Safire, the article was saying this is the real difficulty with not having press conferences, that a process through which they are prepared for by the President was not being experienced by him.

SCHERER: For the record I'd just like to review, briefly, our recommendations of almost a year ago. One, the President should have a regular monthly press conference available for live television coverage and open to all reporters; and, two, in addition, the President should have weekly, informal meetings with reporters in a setting of his choice, with or without radio and television equipment. We do get credit, I think, for helping him to calm it down by recommending that people stay seated and hold up their hand.

DONOVAN: Did he try the lottery thing once?

SCHERER: He tried the lottery thing once.

DONOVAN: Why didn't they pursue it?

SCHERER: The regulars didn't like it. They said that it was too structured, and too many backbenchers got into it—something like that wasn't it, Carroll?

KILPATRICK: I think that's right.

SCHERER: Yes, we were never hot for a lottery but it was an option that we proposed.

LATIMER: Is it true that there's been some kind of an understanding that presidents usually go along with, that the President always recognizes the AP, the UPI, the three major networks, the *Washington Post*, the *New York Times*, the *L. A. Times*? In short, is there any firm group that can count on being recognized? And, would it be unethical or bad, or is it impractical for them to get together and prepare for a press conference by forming an approach of questions with followups, a sort of cooperative preparation of the press to make some logical continuity of the whole thing?

SCHERER: That's been discussed dozens of times. Reporters talk about it in informal ways, but there's just too much anarchy among the press corps; they could never agree.

KILPATRICK: Is the Virginia governor's press conference televised?

LATIMER: Well, it is open to television, and I was just thinking of the evolution since I started. At that time, the *Times-Dispatch* and the AP and occasionally the UPI were covering the capital. Then it has evolved until now there are six or eight television stations, five or six radio stations, and several newspapers. It has gotten out of hand. Where we used to sit down and naturally talk, once or twice a day, when the governor had a lot of time and interest, it has just become a multiplication of different people and different interests.

KILPATRICK: I think that's part of the problem at the White House. They talked about Reagan sitting down with reporters in Sacramento. I think that it's the structure that's different. It makes it bigger, and it's all televised. I think that's a real problem. But to answer your question, the only ones that are regularly called on are either the AP or the UPI on the opening question. From then on he tends to go to the regulars first and then some of the other people later, but there's no understanding.

THOMPSON: One suggestion that occurs to me is that if we do shift from this heavy emphasis on an all-out militaristic foreign policy to one where Reagan talks more about some kind of compromise and settlement of the arms issue, that's going to require a lot of explanation. You would think somebody's going to have to let the hard-pressed American people know what we're doing in that regard. Another thing, it seems to me we live with what president we have. There's something wrong with every one of them, but it does seem to me that for somebody who is at his best in reading scripts, maybe he could read a script on a more structured discussion with a small group of people—that weekly thing you referred to—if he came in prepared. You did talk about single-subject discussions. If he had the script well in mind then maybe he could do fairly well.

SCHERER: Well, we have to assume they like it the way it is, doing the bare minimum. . . .

DONOVAN: George made a point earlier that I would like to ask you about. You belittle, and I understand that, the suggestion that a press conference is the equivalent of a parliamentary debate. It's often been said that the press is the only organ that has a chance to query the president. Isn't there any truth in that?

JUERGENS: I think there's some truth to it. I just think that to draw a direct parallel is too strong. Press conferences occur at the pleasure of the President; if they don't please him, they simply don't occur. The parliamentary question period is built into the system and it occurs at the pleasure of Parliament. It's not up to the Prime Minister whether or not he or she wants to go along. The Prime Minister will appear. I think that there is an important difference also in who's asking the questions. Bear in mind that during the parliamentary question period the questions are coming from elected officials who are performing a constitutional function in asking them. In putting the questions, they are filling a role central to how that system of democracy works. The questions in the United States come from reporters, and reporters you can brush aside a lot easier. I could go on and on with the differences. Now, I think there was a time—and it's hard to date, but more or less from FDR to Eisenhower—when press conferences came as close as anything we have had to serving an equivalent function. But I think they have long since ceased to serve that function.

DONOVAN: Why?

JUERGENS: I think television changed them profoundly.

DONOVAN: All that much?

JUERGENS: I think so. Even the sort of things we were speaking about before: How do you suppose it went over in Podunk or whatever?

DONOVAN: But aren't the same questions being asked that would be asked without television present?

JUERGENS: No. For example, one of the things that is pointed out—I'm making up the numbers, but I'm close—is that the press averaged seven or eight words in asking Roosevelt questions, and about thirty-eight words in asking Kennedy questions. It's not that reporters were necessarily playing to the camera. But since they were terribly aware of the audience out there and didn't know how much the audience knew, to give meaning to their questions they had to start off with long background on what they were talking about. Things became mushier. I think the whole nature of the process changed.

DONOVAN: Well, I'm puzzled about that. I was very much opposed, myself, to all the television in the press conference, and I think Kennedy wrecked it, in a way, by turning it into a matinee. I remember one day when a bunch of nuns were applauding—in a press conference! But, I come back to the question in my own mind: Are these conferences now so really different from what they were? I'm not sure that they are.

JUERGENS: Well, of course, you've experienced both sorts, so in fact you're in a better position to say than I am.

KILPATRICK: Bob, I think they have changed some. I can't express it, but it seems to me there was more informality and follow-up and ease of question and ease of answer, when you were not on television.

DONOVAN: This is partly explained by the growing number of people in the press conference.

KILPATRICK: That's true.

DONOVAN: It's hard to get a question in sometimes.

KILPATRICK: The time limit is another factor. You always have to cut it off at a certain time. Roosevelt sometimes had the press in for only five minutes, but sometimes it lasted forty-five.

DONOVAN: I'm sure the President doesn't forget.

SCHERER: I think what we're simply saying here is there is a great yearning to go back to the Roosevelt informality and the certain element of camaraderie around the desk. But, that's probably impossible. Even if he does hold "pencils-only" news conferences, because of the size of the news corps. . . . We can yearn for it, we can recommend it, but whether or not it would work. . . . The size, and the change in temperament is another thing.

THOMPSON: This has been very profitable and useful for all of us. Just in case you think this area has any difficulties, I ought to report that your successor commission, struggling with the presidential nominating process, has some problems that at least are the equal to the ones you're grappling with now. Its report is a worthy comparison piece to the press study.

CONCLUSION

Knowledge is comparatively limited on the relationship of particular presidents and the press. For example, Robert Donovan in preparation for the Miller Center colloquium discovered he had not written on "Truman and the Press" in his classic two volume biography. He found it was necessary to do additional research culling through notes and sources to write his essay for the current volume. Professor Juergens has written explicitly on Wilson's relation with the press but he is the exception. Few scholars who have written authoritative works on particular presidents have concerned themselves with the press.

It is this gap in presidential literature that the present volume is intended to narrow. We hope that by throwing the spotlight on particular presidents in, contradistinction with presidents in general, we can add to understanding. It may be that the discussion will also enrich that body of writings which concern the media and the public.

In conclusion, the Center's efforts in this sphere have been dependent on the generous assistance of Lloyd Morrisett and the trustees of the John and Mary R. Markle Foundation. Without their encouragement and support, the Miller Center could not have embarked on the studies, lectures, commission reports and colloquia conducted over the past two years.

REPORT OF THE COMMISSION ON PRESIDENTIAL PRESS CONFERENCES

WHITE BURKETT MILLER CENTER OF PUBLIC AFFAIRS UNIVERSITY OF VIRGINIA

Preface

The history of the Miller Center project on the Presidential Press Conference had its origins in discussions in the autumn of 1979 between Mr. Lloyd N. Morrisett, President of the John and Mary R. Markle Foundation, and Professor Kenneth W. Thompson, Director of the Miller Center. The Foundation and the Center share a common interest in communication among the president, the press and the public, and in the improvement of public understanding. The Center had launched its review of the subject in a Forum conducted by Mr. Ray Scherer, Vice President of RCA and formerly White House correspondent of the National Broadcasting Corporation, which was subsequently published in *The Virginia Papers on the Presidency*. Officers of the Markle Foundation expressed interest in the Forum and generously provided funding for a further investigation of the topic.

The staff of the Center first organized interviews and round-tables with a broad cross-section of White House correspond-ents and press secretaries organized into two groups. In stage one of the project, the staff interviewed participants in press conferences conducted by Presidents Franklin D. Roosevelt, Harry S. Truman and Dwight D. Eisenhower, with more limited attention to those of Herbert Hoover and Calvin Coolidge, drawing on the first-hand knowledge of living correspondents. In stage two, the staff turned its attention to the live televised press conferences of Presidents John F. Kennedy, Lyndon B. Johnson, Richard M. Nixon, Gerald R. Ford and Jimmy Carter. The review called attention to the growth of the White House press corps, greater specialization by reporters (including full-time coverage of the White House) and the impact of television on the press conference.

In the next phase of the project, a National Commission, cochaired by Mr. Scherer and Governor Linwood Holton, was created to examine and study the information collected in the first stages of the project and to make recommendations on the future of the presidential press conference. The cochairmen selected members of the Commission, who proceeded to consider whether the presidential press conference, having undergone important changes, continued to serve useful purposes, and sought to define these purposes. The Commission set out to prepare a report based on the preceding discussions, setting forth the origins, evolution and present functioning of the press conference. It undertook to weigh changes and modifications which might lead to improvements, as well as alternatives to the present format.

The Miller Center looks forward to other activities based on the project, including publication of a separate monograph by a Miller Center scholar, followup discussions and colloquia, and the maintenance of archival materials on presidential press conferences. Other projects relating to the president and the press are contemplated.

Acknowledgments

The officers of the Miller Center are indebted to numerous individuals for contributions of inestimable value during the course of the project. Governor Linwood Holton, the Chairman of the Council of the Miller Center, encouraged the staff to embark on the project and graciously agreed to serve as cochairman of the Commission. Mr. Ray Scherer gave intellectual leadership from the outset of the effort. Robert J. Harris, Professor Emeritus of the Department of Government and Foreign Affairs of the University of Virginia was the first staff member to call attention to the importance of the subject. The project would have been impossible without the wholehearted cooperation and assistance of the reporters and press secretaries listed in the appendix. Their dedication to the public interest in seeking to illuminate the central issues of the contemporary press conference was exemplary.

The draft report was written by the extraordinarily able editor of the *Virginia Quarterly Review*, and Special Assistant to the President of the University of Virginia, Mr. Staige Blackford. Mr. Blackford, who had served as press secretary to Governor Holton, brought first-hand knowledge of the process of press conferences to the study. Mr. David Clinton, a staff member of the Miller Center, skillfully prepared and coordinated revisions to the draft report proposed in Commission meetings. Mr. Clyde Lutz assumed full responsibility for the management and administration of the project. Professor James Sterling Young, Director of the Presidency Project at the Center, participated in all the discussions. Mrs. Shirley Kingsbury, Mrs. Cynthia Miller and Mrs. Catherine Stanley faithfully met all deadlines in preparing working memoranda and the report of the Commission.

Above all, we are indebted to Lloyd Morrisett and Mary Milton of the John and Mary R. Markle Foundation. Without their confidence, the project could not have been undertaken.

Their encouragement, both intellectual and material, enabled the effort to go forward. At the same time, in the spirit of private philanthrophy at its best, they respected the independence of participants in the project freely to pursue their inquiries.

We also wish to express our appreciation to the following individuals and organizations. Although this report does not necessarily reflect their views, their generous assistance was essential to its completion: Ms. Blaire French, University of Virginia; Dr. George Gallup, the Gallup Poll; Ms. Gale Mattox, Miller Center; Professor Frederick Mosher, Miller Center; Mr. Jody Powell, White House Press Secretary; Mr. James Reston, Washington Bureau Chief, the *New York Times*; the Honorable Dean Rusk, University of Georgia; Congressional Press Galleries; RCA Corporation; Reporters' Committee for Freedom of the Press; Washington Journalism Center; the White House, State Department, and Defense Department Press Offices.

We believe the present project would have pleased the founder of the Center, Mr. Burkett Miller of Chattanooga, Tennessee. Mr. Miller had a vision of a Center which would contribute both to the advancement of knowledge and to the improvement of the presidency. We would like to think our review of presidential press conferences might prove helpful in both these respects.

REPORT OF THE
COMMISSION ON PRESIDENTIAL
PRESS CONFERENCES
−November 20, 1980−

Introduction

This report deals with the problems and suggested reforms of the presidential press conference.[1] While we are not calling for sweeping changes, we have felt it worthwhile to formulate and publish these proposals for the following reasons: First, the age of electronic communications has radically transformed the press conference, making it a much more public event. Second, despite these changes, the importance of frequency and regularity in holding press conferences has remained. Press conferences derive their credibility from the regularity with which they are scheduled, yet recent presidents have held them only irregularly, to the detriment of all. Third, the press, although it has as great a stake in the operation of the press conference as anyone, has been unable to arrive at recommendations to deal with these problems. Competitive pressures and other factors have made it impossible for the rugged individuals of the Fourth Estate to come to a consensus on reforms.

Thus, the great technological changes that have taken place in the setting of the press conference, the damaging effects of its scheduling in recent years, and the lack of other agreed-upon responses to these developments all led the members of this Commission to believe that they could make a contribution to

---

[1] In this report, the Commission is employing the term "press" to include all forms of mass communication, broadcasting as well as print.

the current discussion of presidential-press relations by collectively advancing some suggestions.

The Presidential Press Conference: A State of Disrepair

"If there is ever to be an amelioration of the condition of
mankind," John Adams observed in 1815, "philosophers, theo-
logians, politicians, and moralists will find that the regulation
of the press is the most difficult, dangerous, and important
problem they have to resolve. Mankind cannot now be governed
without it, nor at present with it." While the First Amendment
to the Constitution specifically forbids any law "abridging the
freedom . . . of the press," and while such freedom is one of the
glories of our heritage and our history, the problem about
which Adams expressed concern 165 years ago, long before the
birth of radio and television, is no less difficult, dangerous, and
important today. It is difficult not only because government is
far more complex but also because the news media have become truly mass, both in the pervasiveness of their message
and in the multitude of those who spread it (2661 news gathering organizations in Washington alone). It is dangerous because
despite all their numbers, despite all their technological magic,
news organizations right now have a standing with the American people, as one distinguished commentator has observed,
somewhere between that of undertakers and used car salesmen;
freedom of the press is less cherished and fear of the press
more widespread. It is important because the security of our
institutions and the survival of our liberties depend, perhaps
more than ever before, on a well-informed public.

The dimensions of this persisting problem are vast, and it is
neither the desire nor the duty of this Commission to examine
them all. We do feel, however, that one of the most important
avenues of communication in this land runs from 1600 Penn-
sylvania Avenue to the rest of America, from the White House
to Main Street. We further feel—and with good reason—that
this avenue has, in recent years, been beset by detours, pocked
with potholes, and cluttered with rubble; hence it is currently
in a state of distressing disrepair.

Yet this state need not be permanent. On the contrary, ours
is a most favorable time to commence the work of repair. The
heat and passion of an election year have subsided, a new
president has been elected, and the climate is propitious for

new ideas, new initiatives and new departures. Moreover, there is every indication that the American people, however great their alleged cynicism and distrust of government, long for a restoration of confidence. Clearly the people are looking for leadership in which they can have belief, faith and hope. And at the pinnacle of American leadership stands the president.

There are, of course, many ways in which a president can *exert* leadership. Equally important, a president must *express* leadership. Surely, one of the best means for such expression is the presidential press conference, where the chief executive has the opportunity to answer questions directly, somewhat as a British prime minister does during the traditional "question period" in the House of Commons. Since an American president, unlike a British prime minister to the Commons, is not answerable to the Congress, the press conference is a significant process of communication: it not only offers the expression of leadership; it also serves the people's right to know. Still, if the people have a right to know and the press is the means by which they can gain that knowledge, members of the press, in turn, have a responsibility to conduct themselves with dignity and decorum. This problem is compounded by the fact that "the press" is not a monolithic institution. It has no hierarchy, no chain of command by which standards of behavior may be enforced. Yet the issue of the behavior of participants in the press conference must be addressed. Otherwise, the process, a delicate one at best, breaks down; and the interests of all—the president, the media, and the people—suffer accordingly. That breakdown has occurred in recent years.

No one party in particular is to blame for this breakdown in communications, yet all involved share some of the guilt. Too often, particularly in the Vietnam and Watergate years, the president has appeared to many observers devious and distrusted in his relations with reporters. Some reporters, their numbers swelled to record proportions, have on occasion demonstrated more an instinct for the jugular than for journalism. Under these circumstances, in an atmosphere of mutual dislike, rather than providing any clarity about the issues of our time, press conferences have sometimes conveyed only confusion; despite their positive features they have at times collapsed into a babble of sound and fury informing nobody. Finally, the public's expectations have been too great. A presidential press conference, however long and however frequent, cannot answer all the questions or solve all the problems, much as many Americans seem to expect.

What then can be done to improve the present precarious condition of the presidential press conference? Obviously, as a physician must "heal thyself," so the healing here must be largely done by the president, aided by the press secretary and the reporters assigned to cover the White House. But there may be a role in the healing process for a group of outside, objective and qualified observers, and that is the reason for this Commission. Asked to serve by the White Burkett Miller Center of Public Affairs, itself charged with the study of the presidency in all its aspects, the Commission's members do not consider themselves strangers to public affairs—or to the White House itself. James Rowe, for one, has a history of public service dating back to his years as a member of Franklin D. Roosevelt's staff. Carroll Kilpatrick, for another, was a White House correspondent during a period spanning the administrations of Roosevelt and Gerald R. Ford. Douglass Cater, for a third, was the Washington editor for *The Reporter* magazine before becoming a special assistant to Lyndon B. Johnson. The Commission's cochairmen are, respectively, a former Virginia governor and assistant secretary of state, Linwood Holton, and a former NBC White House correspondent now vice president of RCA, Ray Scherer. Julius Duscha and Robert Pierpoint are old hands on the Potomac beat, while Felicia Warburg Rogan has long been active in journalistic and community endeavors in New York City and Charlottesville.

The Commission began its deliberations at the outset of last summer and has since held a series of meetings in Washington and Charlottesville. The purpose of these meetings, some of them daylong, was to explore the whole question of the president and the news media with past and present White House correspondents as well as several past presidential press secretaries and staff assistants. Each meeting was taped, and the transcripts of the tapes run to more than 400 pages. Additional research material and assistance were provided by the staff of the Miller Center under the able guidance of its director, Kenneth W. Thompson. At its penultimate meeting in Charlottesville in early October, the Commission decided to limit its recommendations to the press conference alone, without getting into such matters as the media's varying requirements (e.g., those of a newsmagazine vis-a-vis a wire service or a television network, dinners for selected reporters like those in Eisenhower's time or one-on-one TV interviews a la Cronkite, Chancellor, and Walters). Two points should be emphasized: 1) the Commission is not acting alone from the vantage point of some lofty ivory tower; it has had the generous assistance and advice of those who have participated in White House press conferences since the administration of Calvin Coolidge; and 2) the Commission does not offer its recommendations as the be-all and end-all solutions to the conduct of presidential press conferences, but rather as suggestions as to how the conduct—and accordingly the product—of such conferences can be improved. A final point is this: we are not so naive as to think our recommendations will be received with reverence but we would trust that our report will be given the care and consideration which went into its making. We offer our suggestions fully cognizant that the press conference is the president's prerogative. There is nothing in the Constitution which directs him to meet reporters. He can lay down any rules he wishes. He can even choose to hold no press conferences at all. We are not directing him in this report to do anything. Again, we ask only that it be considered. Before offering our recommendations, however, we believe that a short history of the presidential press conference is in order, and it constitutes the next section of this document.

The Presidential Press Conference: A Brief History

The presidential press conference is an institution whose long and distinguished history has given it a prominent place in the American political firmament. Although earlier presidents may on occasion have had casual meetings with editors and reporters, the press conference as such is a phenomenon of the twentieth century. For eighty years presidents have, in one forum or another, answered questions from reporters in an effort to communicate with both the news media and the public at large. Theodore Roosevelt first brought groups of reporters into the White House for interviews from time to time—often while he was being shaved in the morning. After a four-year lapse during the Taft administration, the press conference returned in 1913 to Woodrow Wilson's White House, where it has since remained. Wilson introduced the practices of regular meetings with the press and equal access for all accredited reporters to conferences. Warren Harding, Calvin Coolidge, and Herbert Hoover continued these sessions, although they required that questions be submitted in writing to them in advance.

With the presidency of Franklin Roosevelt, the press conference entered its most productive, and perhaps most colorful, era. Roosevelt's conferences contained very little that was wholly new; submission to a spontaneous question-and-answer period, a willingness to speak off-the-record and provide extensive background information, and the availability of direct presidential quotes to reporters were all devices that had been used previously by one president or another. But Roosevelt's skillful mixing of all these elements when he met with one hundred or so reporters gathered around his desk gave the press conferences of his day a distinctive flavor—informal yet informative— which they had not enjoyed before and which they have rarely recaptured since.

Over the past thirty-five years, the press conference as an institution had continued to evolve, responding to continuing changes in communications, most particularly the advent of television, and in the American political system. With the United States emerging as a superpower from World War II and Washington becoming the capital of the so-called Free World, the number of reporters attending White House press conferences increased enormously. As a result, Harry Truman had no choice but to stand before the assembled reporters rather than speak to them as they clustered about his desk, and much of the Rooseveltian air of intimacy was lost. Radio taping and, to a greater extent, television filming for delayed airing inaugurated under Dwight Eisenhower, made it more difficult for presidents to provide extensive background information off-the-record. They also became more reluctant to speak freely, fearful of being caught in a slip of the tongue. The decision to televise press conferences live, made by John F. Kennedy, accelerated these trends. Projected in black-and-white, later in "living color," a president was directly in the public eye and seemed to feel that he could neither seek a delay for more information nor say, "No comment." Kennedy's immediate successors only contributed to a worsening in relations between the president and the members of the Fourth Estate (or what one member of this Commission has called "the Fourth Branch of Government"). What many in the press regarded as deceptions, as with Lyndon Johnson's reports about the Vietnam War and Richard Nixon's duplicities about Watergate, raised a curtain of distrust between the president and the press. If the role of the news media in their relationship to the White House had hitherto been adversarial, it now became downright antagonistic.

Meanwhile, the presidential press conference turned into a shouting contest among reporters for the president's eye. Although reporters had clamored for attention before, the presence of television added a new dimension to the turmoil of the press conference. And such conditions continued to prevail, for the most part, under Gerald Ford and Jimmy Carter, with reporters jumping and yelling for attention like children on a playground. Thus *Broadcasting* magazine was prompted to headline its September 29, 1980 story announcing the formation of this Commission, "Trying to Create Order Out of Chaos."

The Presidential Press Conference: Recommendations

Creating order from chaos does not have to be a monumental undertaking, provided there is a willingness on the part of both parties, the president and the news media, to agree a) that the status quo is unacceptable and should not be continued, and b) that some give-and-take from each side is required to make the necessary innovations and/or improvements. We believe that such a willingness may exist, and we therefore trust that our recommendations will not be consigned to that great dustbin of unread proposals. Our proposals may seem almost too simple at first glance, but they can, we unanimously believe, be of benefit to all concerned—the president, the media, and most of all, the American people.

The key to the success of any presidential press conference relationship is frequency. The more often a president meets reporters, the greater the interchange, the less chance there is for communication to break down. We are encouraged by President-elect Reagan's declaration at his November 6 post-election Los Angeles press conference to "do our best to have them on a fairly regular and consistent basis."

Our recommendations are these: 1) the president should have a *regular monthly* press conference available for live television coverage and open to all reporters; and 2) in addition, the president should have weekly informal meetings with reporters in a setting of his choice, with or without radio and television equipment. Here we reprint with commendation the opening remarks made by Franklin Roosevelt at his first presidential press conference on March 8, 1933:

THE PRESIDENT: It is very good to see you all. My hope is that these conferences are going to be merely enlarged editions of the kind of very delightful family conferences I have been holding in Albany for the last four years.

I am told that what I am about to do will become impossible, but I am going to try it. We are not going to have any more written questions; and, of course, while I cannot answer seventy-five or a hundred questions because I simply haven't got the time, I see no reason why I should not talk to you ladies and gentlemen off the record in just the way I have been doing in Albany and in the way I used to do in the Navy Department down here. Quite a number of you, I am glad to see, date back to the days of the previous existence which I led in Washington.

And so I think we shall discontinue the practice of compelling the submitting of questions in writing before the conference in order to get an answer. There will be a great many questions, of course, that I won't answer, either because they are "if" questions—and I never answer them—and Brother Stephenson will tell you what an "if" question is—

MR. STEPHENSON (Reporter): I ask forty of them a day.

THE PRESIDENT: And the others, of course, are the questions which for various reasons I do not want to discuss, or I am not ready to discuss, or I do not know anything about. There will be a great many questions you will ask that I do not know enough about to answer.

Then, in regard to news announcements, Steve (Early, Assistant Secretary to the President) and I thought that it would be best that straight news for use from this office should always be without direct quotations. In other words, I do not want to be directly quoted, unless direct quotations are given out by Steve in writing. That makes that perfectly clear.

Then there are two other matters we will talk about: The first is "background information," which means material which can be used by all of you on your own authority and responsibility, not to be attributed to the White House, because I do not want to have to revive the Ananias Club. (Laughter)

Then the second thing is the "off the record" information which means, of course, confidential information which is given only to those who attend the conference. Now there is one thing I want to say right now about which I think you will go along with me. I want to ask you not to repeat this "off the record" confidential information either to your own editors or to your associates who are not here; because there is always the danger that, while you people may not violate the rule, somebody may forget to say, "This is off the record and confidential," and the other party may use it in a story. That is to say, it is not to be used and not to be told to those fellows who happen not to come around to the conference. In other words, it is only for those present.[2]

We believe that these ground rules provide the best opportunity for the two types of press conferences to serve their somewhat different purposes. The formal conference lets the president communicate directly with the people of America and of the world; it also serves the important symbolic function of displaying a president's continuing mental and physical vigor, as shown by the ability to handle a series of unrehearsed and probing questions with the nation as witness. The informal weekly conference is an opportunity for more reflective, candid discussions of issues and events. It allows the president to educate the public indirectly; and, by providing reporters with the necessary background on important topics, it enables them to ask more informed questions which better protect the public's right to know.

To the argument that weekly informal meetings and at least one large televised conference a month are too much of a demand on a president's time, we might point out that Roosevelt—hardly an inactive executive, and president during

---

[2]*The Public Papers and Addresses of Franklin D. Roosevelt*, 13 vols. (New York: Random House, 1938), 11:30–31.

the difficult Depression and war years—met the press twice a week. And both Truman and Eisenhower regularly held sessions once a week; it is only in the past twenty years that the frequency and regularity of press conferences have declined. Furthermore, meeting reporters more frequently and more informally might give them a better comprehension of what the president is seeking to attain and the president a better idea of what issues concern the public. More frequent meetings might also help the president to better understand the demands on the media and the media to better comprehend the demands on the president, thereby retaining the traditional adversary relationship between government and the media without so much antagonism getting involved.

The manner in which presidential press conferences are presently conducted on live television—with reporters jumping up, waving their hands, and shouting, "Mr. President! Mr. President!" in an effort to gain the president's eye and the opportunity to ask a question—is what so many viewers (and participants) find appalling. The easiest remedy for this requires little more than an exercise in presidential leadership: the president could enforce order by refusing to acknowledge or answer any reporter who shouts. He answers only those who raise their hand and allows follow-up questions.

Another option which might be considered would be to have the questioners at a televised press conference chosen by lot. This has worked well on presidential trips out of Washington. Reporters desiring to ask a question would submit their names—but not their questions—in advance of the conference. Those chosen in a system of random selection would be listed in the order picked and the list posted, with a copy going to the president, who would then call those on the list and allow each questioner a follow-up question. At least two exceptions could be made: the Associated Press and the United Press International correspondents would retain their traditional right to ask the first two questions.

To those who say the president benefits in the eyes of the public from what is now perceived as a confrontation with the arrogant and obstreperous behavior of correspondents, we would offer an eloquent rebuttal made by British author Godfrey Hodgson in his new book, *All Things To All Men: The*

False Promise of the Modern American Presidency. In his chapter on the president and the media, entitled "The Electronic Mephistopheles," Hodgson concludes: "The media's interest in the President seems increasingly tinged with cynicism. The public seems increasingly skeptical and indifferent. A cycle of diminishing returns seems underway, perhaps irreversibly so."

Although we believe the last, best salvation for a modern president is the exercise of effective leadership—and leadership he clearly enjoys exercising—we cite Mr. Hodgson to show that the president has something, in fact a great deal, to gain by getting away from the circus-like atmosphere of today's press conferences.

There is much to be said for renewing the informal gathering of correspondents that took place during the 1930s and 1940s. We realize, of course, that the size of the present news corps precludes gathering around the president's desk. But we see no reason why the president cannot have a weekly informal meeting with reporters. In some circumstances, the president could speak for attribution but not for direct quotation—"The president said." Reporters would, though, have the right to check with the press secretary in certain instances to see if the president would permit a quote.

So we hold that these innovations, a minimum of one monthly live TV conference, with a better method of questioning, and weekly informal meetings, can have a substantial and significant benefit.

We hope these recommendations will be received as we have endeavored to formulate them—thoughtfully, thoroughly and sincerely. We do not offer these proposals as though they were engraved in marble and not subject to further contemplation and change; nor do we assert that the ideas which underlie them are wholly new or original. We do offer them secure in our belief that if there is a will to explore them, there is a way to turn them into realities.

The Presidential Press Conference: An Afterword

We opened this report with a quotation from one of America's founding fathers. We close with a quotation from another, one intimately involved with the institution of which the Miller

Center is a part—the University of Virginia. For that institution, the Virginian who is so much its father had many great expectations. And one of the expectations Thomas Jefferson envisaged for his university was this: "... here we are not afraid to follow the truth wherever it may lead, nor to tolerate any error so long as reason is left free to combat it." That, we submit, is the standard to which all involved in the presidential press conference must adhere.

Linwood Holton, cochairman
Douglass Cater
Julius Duscha
Carroll Kilpatrick

Ray Scherer, cochairman
Robert Pierpoint
James Rowe
Felicia Warburg Rogan

Bibliography

Bagdikian, Ben. *The Effete Conspiracy*. New York: Harper and Row, 1972.

Carter, Jimmy. *Public Papers of the President*. Washington, D.C.: National Archives and Records Service.

Cater, Douglass. *The Fourth Branch of Government*. Boston: Houghton Mifflin Company, 1959.

Cornwell, Elmer E., Jr. *Presidential Leadership of Public Opinion*. Bloomington, Indiana: Indiana University Press, 1966.

Crouse, Timothy, *The Boys on the Bus*. New York: Random House, 1973.

Eisenhower, Dwight D. *Public Papers of the President*. Washington, D.C.: National Archives and Records Service.

Ford, Gerald R. *A Time to Heal*. New York: Harper and Row, 1979.

_____. *Public Papers of the President*. Washington, D.C.: National Archives and Records Service.

Grossman, Michael and Martha Kumar. "Milton's Army: The White House Press Corps." Paper prepared for delivery at the 1979 Annual meeting of the American Political Science Association, August 31 to September 3, 1979.

_____. "The Media and the Presidency: An Exchange Analysis." *Political Science Quarterly*. Spring, 1979.

Halberstam, David. "Press and Prejudice." *Esquire*. April, 1974.

Hess, Stephen. *Organizing the Presidency*. Washington, D.C.: The Brookings Institution, 1976.

Hodgson, Godfrey. *All Things to All Men: The False Promise of the Modern American Presidency*. New York: Simon and Schuster, 1980.

Hoover, Herbert. *Public Papers of the President*. Washington, D.C.: National Archives and Records Service.

Johnson, Lyndon. *Public Papers of the President*. Washington, D.C.: National Archives and Records Service.

_____. *The Johnson Presidential Press Conferences*. Editor, Doris Kearns. Volumes 1 and 2. New York: Earl M. Coleman Enterprises, Inc., 1978.

Kennedy, John F. *Public Papers of the President*. Washington, D.C.: National Archives and Records Service.

Keogh, James. *President Nixon and the Press*. New York: Funk and Wagnalls, 1972.

Lammers, William W. "Presidential Press Conference Schedules: Who Hides, And When?" Paper prepared for delivery at the 1979 Annual Meeting of the American Political Science Association, August 31 to September 3, 1979

Moore, Susan E. "Presidential Press Conferences." Freedom of Information Center Report No. 339. July, 1975.

Moynihan, Daniel P. "The Presidency and the Press." *Commentary*. March, 1971.

Nixon, Richard M. *Public Papers of the President*. Washington, D.C.: National Archives and Records Service.

_____. *The Nixon Presidential Press Conferences*. Editor, David Halberstam. New York: Earl M. Coleman Enterprises, Inc., 1978.

Perry, James. *Us and Them*. New York: Clarkson N. Potter, 1973.

Pollard, James E. "The News Conference As A Communication Channel." *The Public Opinion Quarterly*. Winter 1951–1952.

_____. *The Presidents and the Press*. New York: Macmillan, 1974.

_____. *The Presidents and the Press: Truman to Johnson*. Washington, D.C.: Public Affairs Press, 1964.

The Presidency and the Press Conference. Rational Debate Seminars. Washington, D.C.: American Enterprise Institute for Public Policy Research, 1971.

Purvis, Hoyt, Editor. *The Presidency and the Press*. Austin, Texas: The University of Texas at Austin, 1976.

Reedy, George. *The Twilight of the Presidency*. New York: Columbia University Press, 1970.

Reston, James. *The Artillery of the Press: Its Influence on American Foreign Policy*. New York: Harper and Row, 1967.

Rivers, William. *The Adversaries*. Boston: Beacon Press, 1970.

Roosevelt, Franklin D. *Complete Presidential Press Conferences of Franklin D. Roosevelt*. New York: De Capo Press, 1972.

_____. *Franklin D. Roosevelt: Selected Speeches, Messages, Press Conferences, and Letters*. New York: Holt, Rinehart and Winston, 1964.

Sallinger, Pierre. *With Kennedy*. Garden City, N.Y.: Doubleday and Co., 1966.

Scherer, Ray. "The Presidential Press Conference." *The Virginia Papers On The Presidency: The White Burkett Miller Center Forums, 1979*. Editor, Kenneth Thompson. Washington, D.C.: University Press of America, Inc., 1979.

Small, William J. *Political Power and the Press*. New York: W.W. Norton, 1972.

Smith, Hedrick. "When The President Meets The Press." *Atlantic*. August, 1970.

Smith, Merriman. *Thank You, Mr. President: A White House Notebook*. New York: Harper and Brothers Publishers, 1946.

Stein, M. L. *When Presidents Meet the Press*. New York: Julian Messmer, 1969.

Truman, Harry. *Public Papers of the President*. Washington, D.C.: National Archives and Records Service.

Wise, David. *The Politics of Lying*. New York: Random House, 1973.

Witcover, Jules. "How Well Does the White House Press Perform?" *Columbia Journalism Review*. November/December, 1973.

_____. "Salvaging the Presidential Press Conference." *Columbia Journalism Review*. Fall, 1970.

Wolfson, Lewis W. "A Report on the State of the Presidential Press Conference." New York: The National News Council, 1975.

_____. et al. *The Press Covers Government: The Nixon Years from 1969 to Watergate*. Washington, D.C.: American University/National Press Club, 1973.

Participants in Earlier
Background Meetings

Mr. Lawrence Burd, former White House Correspondent, *Chicago Tribune*
Mr. Douglass Cater, Aspen Institute
Professor James W. Ceaser, University of Virginia
Mr. Frank Cormier, White House Correspondent, United Press International
Mr. Kenneth G. Crawford, former columnist, *Newsweek*
Mr. James Deakin, White House Correspondent, *St. Louis Post-Dispatch*
Mr. Robert J. Donovan, former Washington Bureau Chief, New York *Herald-Tribune* and *Los Angeles Times*
Mr. Julius C. Duscha, Washington Journalism Center
Professor Michael Grossman, Towson State College
The Honorable Linwood Holton, Vice President and General Counsel, American Council of Life Insurance; Chairman, Miller Center Council
Mr. Carroll Kilpatrick, White House Correspondent, *Washington Post*
Professor Martha Kumar, Towson State College
Mr. Ronald H. Nessen, Press Secretary, President Ford
Mr. Jerry O'Leary, White House Correspondent, *Washington Star*
Mr. James Rowe, Special Assistant, President Roosevelt
Mr. Ray Scherer, Vice President, RCA Corporation; former White House Correspondent, NBC News
Professor Kenneth W. Thompson, Director, Miller Center of Public Affairs
Mr. Roger W. Tubby, Press Secretary, President Truman
Mr. Sander Vanocur, former White House Correspondent, NBC News; Vice President, Special Reporting Units, ABC News
Professor James S. Young, Director, Program on the Presidency, Miller Center of Public Affairs